Fast Track to Freedom

Fast Track to Freedom

30 DAYS TO FINANCIAL INDEPENDENCE USING AI, ASSETS, AND AGILE HUSTLES

Matthew Petchinsky

Apophis Enterprises LLC

1

∽

Fast Track to Freedom: 30 Days to Financial Independence Using AI, Assets, and Agile Hustles
By: Matthew Petchinsky

Part I: Setting the Stage for Financial Freedom

Chapter 1: The Blueprint to Financial Freedom

Understanding Financial Freedom and the Mindset Needed

Financial freedom is a stage in life where you are no longer required to work for a living but choose to work on what you love, invest, or create further wealth because of your financial stability. Achieving this freedom means that your assets generate income that exceeds your expenses. It's not merely about being wealthy, but about gaining the autonomy to make choices in life without the constraints of financial pressure.

The Essence of Financial Freedom

To understand financial freedom, it's essential to grasp the difference between financial independence and financial abundance. Financial independence occurs when you have sufficient wealth to live on without working, while financial abundance refers to having more money than you ever need. Financial freedom sits comfortably between these two, focusing not just on surviving but thriving.

The Right Mindset for Achieving Financial Freedom

The journey to financial freedom starts with the right mindset. This involves:

- **Self-Awareness**: Knowing what truly matters to you—differentiating between wants and needs.
- **Goal-Oriented Planning**: Setting clear, achievable goals (short-term and long-term) and visualizing the steps to achieve them.

- **Resilience**: Being prepared for setbacks and viewing failures as stepping stones rather than obstacles.
- **Lifelong Learning**: Committing to continuous education and adaptation, especially in fast-evolving fields like technology and finance.
- **Risk Management**: Understanding how to assess and take calculated risks, and not shying away from them when necessary.

Adopting a mindset that embraces these principles will set a solid foundation for your journey to financial freedom.

Overview of the 30-Day Plan

The "Fast Track to Freedom" program is structured around a 30-day plan designed to kickstart your journey toward financial independence using three powerful tools: AI, assets, and agile hustles. Each of these components plays a crucial role in building your financial blueprint.

Week 1: Setting the Foundation
- **Day 1-3**: Self-Assessment and Goal Setting. Define what financial freedom means to you and set realistic financial goals.
- **Day 4-6**: Financial Education. Learn the basics of personal finance, investing, and the potential of AI in financial planning.
- **Day 7**: Planning. Develop a detailed financial plan that aligns with your goals.

Week 2: Integrating AI and Technology
- **Day 8-10**: Understanding AI Capabilities. Dive into how AI can optimize budgeting, investments, and income streams.
- **Day 11-13**: Implementing AI Tools. Start using AI-based financial tools for budgeting, investing, and earning.
- **Day 14**: Review. Assess the effectiveness of AI tools and adjust your strategy.

Week 3: Building Assets
- **Day 15-17**: Asset Identification. Identify which types of assets (stocks, real estate, business ventures) fit best with your strategy.
- **Day 18-20**: Asset Acquisition Strategies. Learn and begin implementing strategies for acquiring these assets.
- **Day 21**: Evaluation. Review your asset portfolio and its alignment with your financial goals.

Week 4: Agile Hustles
- **Day 22-24**: Exploring Agile Hustles. Identify and explore flexible side hustles that can generate immediate income.
- **Day 25-27**: Implementing Hustles. Start the hustles, using AI to maximize efficiency and profitability.
- **Day 28-30**: Scaling and Review. Evaluate the success of your hustles and plan for scaling or pivoting.

Bringing It All Together
The final day of the plan is dedicated to reviewing the progress made over the past month and adjusting the plan for the upcoming months. It's vital to continually monitor and adapt your strategies based on market conditions, personal growth, and financial performance.

This 30-day plan is designed to provide a solid foundation for anyone looking to achieve financial independence through innovative and proactive measures. By understanding the core concepts, adopting the right mindset, and actively engaging in each step of the plan, you can set yourself on a path to financial freedom.

Chapter 2: Financial Assessment and Goal Setting

Evaluating Your Current Financial Status

To embark on a journey toward financial freedom, you must first understand where you stand financially. This initial assessment is crucial as it provides a clear picture of your current resources, obligations, and overall financial health. This assessment involves several key steps:

Step 1: Calculate Net Worth

Your net worth is the difference between what you own (assets) and what you owe (liabilities). Calculating this gives you a snapshot of your financial health and helps track progress over time.

- **Assets**: Include all savings, investments, properties, and other valuable possessions.
- **Liabilities**: Include all debts such as loans, mortgages, credit card balances, and other financial obligations.

Step 2: Analyze Cash Flow

Understanding your cash flow involves tracking all income and expenses over a typical month. This helps identify spending patterns, wasteful expenses, and potential savings.

- **Income Sources**: Document all sources of income, including salaries, dividends, and any side hustles.
- **Expenses**: Categorize expenses into essentials (rent, utilities, groceries) and non-essentials (dining out, entertainment).

Step 3: Evaluate Debt

High-interest debt can cripple your ability to achieve financial freedom. Assess your debts by listing them along with their interest rates and terms.

• **Strategic Debt Reduction**: Prioritize paying off high-interest debts and consider refinancing options to lower interest rates.

Step 4: Risk Management and Insurance

Review your insurance policies (health, life, property) to ensure adequate coverage. This protects against unforeseen financial setbacks.

Setting Clear, Achievable Financial Goals

Once you have a thorough understanding of your financial status, the next step is to set clear and achievable goals. These goals should be specific, measurable, achievable, relevant, and time-bound (SMART).

Short-Term Goals (1-2 Years)

These might include paying off credit card debt, saving for an emergency fund, or taking a course to improve job skills. Short-term goals are crucial as they provide quick wins and help build momentum.

Mid-Term Goals (3-5 Years)

Mid-term goals may involve saving for a down payment on a home, starting a business, or investing in learning advanced skills. These require more commitment and often involve saving or investing significant amounts.

Long-Term Goals (5 Years and Beyond)

These goals focus on achieving financial independence and might include reaching a net-worth milestone, generating passive income through investments, or fully funding a retirement account.

Utilizing AI and Tech Tools for Financial Planning

To assist in both assessing your current financial status and tracking progress towards your goals, AI and technology offer powerful tools:

- **Budgeting Apps**: Apps like Mint or YNAB can help track income and expenses, offering insights into spending habits and potential savings.
- **Investment Simulators**: AI-driven platforms can simulate various investment scenarios to forecast potential outcomes and suggest optimal investment strategies.
- **Debt Management Tools**: Technologies such as Unbury.Me utilize algorithms to propose the fastest or cheapest strategies for debt repayment based on your financial data.

Conclusion

This chapter lays the groundwork for your financial transformation. By rigorously assessing your current financial situation and setting well-defined, achievable goals, you create a robust foundation for your journey to financial freedom. In the subsequent chapters, we will explore how to leverage AI, acquire valuable assets, and initiate agile hustles to accelerate this journey, making smart, informed financial decisions along the way.

Financial Analysis Spreadsheet Template

1. Setup Your Spreadsheet

Create a spreadsheet with the following columns:

- **Date**: The date of the transaction.
- **Description**: A brief description of the transaction.
- **Category**: The category of the expense or income (e.g., Income, Bills, Essentials, Fuel, Food, Impulse Spending).
- **Amount**: The amount of the transaction.
- **Type**: Whether it's an income or expense.

2. Categories and Subcategories

Define the categories you'll use to track your finances:

- **Income**: All sources of income (salary, freelance, etc.).
- **Bills**: Regular monthly payments (rent, utilities, subscriptions).
- **Essentials**: Necessary spending excluding bills (groceries, household items).
- **Fuel**: Transportation costs including public transport and fuel for personal vehicles.
- **Food**: Includes dining out and other food expenses not covered under essentials.
- **Impulse Spending**: Non-essential expenses that are spontaneous or unplanned.

3. Monthly Summary

At the end of the spreadsheet, create a section to summarize your monthly spending:

- **Total Income**: Sum of all income.
- **Total Bills**: Sum of all bills.
- **Total Essentials**: Sum of essential expenses.
- **Total Fuel**: Sum of all fuel expenses.
- **Total Food**: Sum of all food expenses.
- **Total Impulse Spending**: Sum of impulse spending.
- **Net Savings**: Total Income minus Total Expenses.:

4. Tracking and Analysis

- **Monthly Tracking**: At the end of each month, review your expenses to see where your money is going. This helps in identifying areas where you can cut back.
- **Charts and Graphs**: Use the chart tools in your spreadsheet software to create visual representations of your income vs. expenses, spending by category, and month-over-month trends.

5. Review and Adjust

Regularly review this spreadsheet to ensure your spending aligns with your financial goals. Adjust your budget as necessary to account for changes in income, lifestyle, or financial objectives.

Using the Spreadsheet

Fill in this spreadsheet daily or weekly with your income and expenditures. Over time, this will give you a clear picture of your financial health and help you make informed decisions about where to allocate your money.

Chapter 3: Essential Financial Tools and Resources

Introduction to Financial Planning Tools and Apps

In today's digital age, a myriad of tools and resources are available to aid individuals in achieving financial independence. These tools can simplify complex financial tasks, from budgeting to investing, and provide invaluable insights into your financial health. This chapter will introduce some of the most effective financial planning tools and apps, which can help streamline your path to financial freedom.

Key Financial Planning Tools

1. **Budgeting Apps**: Apps like Mint, YNAB (You Need A Budget), and PocketGuard help users track their spending, set budget limits, and notify them when they're about to exceed these limits. These tools are designed to provide a clear overview of income and expenses, facilitating better financial decisions.

2. **Investment Platforms**: Tools like Robinhood, Acorns, and Betterment make investing accessible and straightforward. These platforms offer user-friendly interfaces and the ability to start investing with small amounts, making them ideal for beginners.

3. **Debt Management Tools**: Apps such as Unbury.Me and Debt Payoff Planner assist in managing and strategizing the repayment of debts. They offer various repayment plans like the Snowball or

Avalanche methods, helping users reduce and eventually eliminate debt.

4. **Credit Monitoring Services**: Services like Credit Karma and Experian provide free credit reports, monitoring, and advice on how to improve your credit score, which is crucial for obtaining favorable loan terms and interest rates.

5. **Financial Planning Software**: More comprehensive tools like Quicken or Personal Capital offer a range of services from budgeting to detailed investment analysis, giving users a holistic view of their financial situation.

How Technology Can Streamline Budgeting and Investments

Technology not only simplifies the management of finances but can also lead to more informed and strategic financial decisions. Here's how technology is revolutionizing budgeting and investing:

Streamlining Budgeting

- **Automated Tracking**: Most budgeting apps connect directly to your bank accounts, credit cards, and other financial accounts to automatically track and categorize spending. This automation saves time and improves accuracy in budget management.
- **Real-Time Alerts**: Real-time notifications alert you about any unusual expenses or when you're nearing your budget limits, helping prevent overspending.
- **Goal Setting**: Digital tools allow for easy setup of savings and spending goals, visually tracking your progress towards these goals, which keeps you motivated and on track.

Enhancing Investments

- **Robo-Advisors**: Using algorithms, robo-advisors such as Wealthfront and Betterment provide personalized investment advice at a lower cost than human advisors. They automatically adjust your portfolio based on changes in the market conditions and your financial goals.

- **AI and Machine Learning**: Advanced AI technologies analyze vast amounts of market data to predict trends and provide investment insights, which were previously only accessible to professional traders.

- **Blockchain and Cryptocurrencies**: Technologies like blockchain introduce new investment opportunities in cryptocurrencies and ICOs (Initial Coin Offerings), which can be lucrative but also require a good understanding of the technology to manage risk effectively.

Conclusion

As technology continues to advance, the array of tools available for financial planning will only grow. Leveraging these tools effectively requires a basic understanding of how they work and what they offer. In this digital era, those who utilize these technologies to their full extent will likely find themselves ahead of the curve in their journey to financial independence. By integrating these digital tools into your financial strategy, as outlined in our 30-day plan, you can enhance your financial literacy, streamline your budgeting and investments, and accelerate your path to financial freedom.

Chapter 4: The Role of Artificial Intelligence in Personal Finance

How AI Can Enhance Financial Decision-Making

Artificial Intelligence (AI) is transforming numerous industries, and personal finance is no exception. AI's ability to analyze large volumes of data quickly and accurately can significantly enhance financial decision-making. In personal finance, AI is used to predict market trends, optimize investment strategies, personalize financial advice, and much more. This chapter explores how AI is specifically enhancing financial decision-making through smarter, faster, and more tailored financial solutions.

Personalized Financial Insights

AI algorithms can analyze your spending habits, income, lifestyle choices, and financial goals to provide personalized insights. For instance, if AI notices that you're frequently incurring overdraft fees, it might recommend better cash flow management strategies or suggest switching to a bank with lower fees and better terms.

Enhanced Risk Management

AI can help identify and assess risk in real-time. For investments, AI tools use predictive analytics to foresee market fluctuations, helping users to manage investment risks more effectively. By analyzing historical and current financial data, AI can suggest when to buy, hold, or sell assets based on individual risk tolerance and financial goals.

Automated Financial Management

Robo-advisors are AI-driven platforms that automate asset management. They provide financial advice and investment management online with minimal human intervention, making financial planning more accessible and less expensive for the average person.

Review of Top AI Tools for Budgeting, Investing, and Saving

The market is replete with AI tools designed to simplify and enhance various aspects of personal finance. Here's a review of some of the top AI tools currently reshaping budgeting, investing, and saving practices.

AI Tools for Budgeting

- **Mint:** This app uses AI to categorize transactions automatically and track spending patterns. It also offers personalized suggestions on how to reduce costs and improve savings.
- **YNAB (You Need A Budget):** YNAB uses AI to provide users with forecasts based on their spending habits, helping them adjust their budgets to save more.
- **PocketGuard:** This app uses AI to optimize spending by identifying recurring bills and suggesting ways to reduce them. It also helps in finding better deals for services like internet and insurance.

AI Tools for Investing

- **Betterment:** One of the first robo-advisors, Betterment uses AI algorithms to manage portfolios based on the user's risk tolerance and time horizon. It adjusts the investment strategy as the market changes and as users approach their financial goals.
- **Wealthfront:** Similar to Betterment, Wealthfront uses AI to provide automated financial planning services. It also includes a feature called PassivePlus, which is a suite of investment strategies that use AI to enhance returns.
- **Ellevest:** Designed specifically for women, Ellevest uses AI to create personalized investment plans that consider gender-specific salary arcs and life spans.

AI Tools for Saving

- **Digit:** This app analyzes your spending habits and automatically transfers money from checking to a savings account based on what you can afford at any given time. It uses machine learning to understand how and when you save money.
- **Qapital:** Qapital uses AI to help users set and achieve specific financial goals through automated rules that trigger transfers to

savings when certain conditions are met (like rounding up to the nearest dollar on purchases).

Conclusion

Artificial Intelligence is not just a technological advancement; it's a tool that can significantly enhance how we manage personal finances. From budgeting and saving to investing and beyond, AI offers opportunities to optimize financial decision-making and achieve financial goals more efficiently. As AI technology continues to evolve, its integration into personal finance tools will likely become more profound, offering even smarter, more intuitive, and highly personalized financial management solutions. This integration is pivotal in the journey towards financial independence and is an essential component of the "Fast Track to Freedom" program.

Part II: Income Generation Strategies

Chapter 5: Profit from AI: Developing and Selling AI Applications

Basics of Creating Simple AI Models

Entering the world of AI development can be a lucrative venture. Even those with minimal coding experience can learn to create simple AI models, thanks to user-friendly platforms and resources. Here's a primer on how to get started.

Understanding AI and Machine Learning

First, it's crucial to understand what AI and machine learning (ML) entail. AI is a broad field that involves creating systems capable of performing tasks that typically require human intelligence. Machine learning is a subset of AI focused on developing algorithms that allow computers to learn from and make decisions based on data.

Learning the Basics

- **Educational Resources**: Websites like Coursera, Udacity, and Khan Academy offer courses in AI and machine learning. Start with introductory courses that don't require a strong background in math or programming.
- **Python**: Python is a popular language in AI development due

to its readability and the wide availability of libraries and frame-works. Libraries like TensorFlow, PyTorch, and Scikit-learn are instrumental in building AI models.

Building Simple AI Models

- **Choose a Problem to Solve**: Begin with a problem that can be addressed through AI. This could be something as straightforward as a recommendation system or a predictive model.
- **Collect and Prepare Data**: AI models require data. You can find datasets on platforms like Kaggle or Google Dataset Search. Data preparation involves cleaning the data and selecting the right features for your model.
- **Model Development**: Use an AI framework to develop your model. This typically involves selecting an algorithm, training the model on your data, and then testing it to see how well it performs.
- **Iteration**: AI development is highly iterative. Continue refining your model based on performance feedback until it meets your standards.

Platforms for Selling or Licensing AI Tools

Once you have developed an AI application, the next step is mone-tization. There are several platforms where you can sell or license your AI tools.

Direct Sales and Licensing

- **Own Website**: Selling or licensing through your own website gives you full control over pricing and customer relations. You can use payment processing systems like Stripe or PayPal to handle transactions.
- **GitHub**: If your AI tool is software-based, GitHub offers a way to host and review code, manage projects, and build software along-side millions of other developers.

Marketplaces and Platforms

- **AWS Marketplace**: A digital catalog with thousands of software listings from independent software vendors that make it easy to find, test, buy, and deploy software that runs on Amazon Web Services (AWS).
- **Microsoft AppSource**: For AI applications that integrate with Microsoft products, this marketplace can help reach a broad audience of business users.
- **Google Cloud Marketplace**: Offers ready-to-go development stacks, solutions, and services to accelerate development on Google Cloud.

Freemium and Subscription Models

- **Freemium Model**: Offer basic features of your AI tool for free while charging for premium features. This model can attract a large user base quickly.
- **Subscription Model**: Charge a recurring fee for access to your AI tool. This model ensures a consistent revenue stream and can be coupled with different tiers of service offerings.

Consulting and Custom Solutions

- **AI Consulting**: Many companies look for tailored AI solutions but lack the expertise to develop them in-house. Offering consulting services can be a profitable way to leverage your AI skills.
- **Custom AI Solutions**: Develop bespoke solutions for specific client needs. This approach often leads to higher margins as you provide a specialized service.

Conclusion

Developing and selling AI applications can be a significant step towards financial independence. By understanding the basics of AI, creating valuable tools, and leveraging the right platforms for sales and licensing, you can tap into the vast potential of the AI market. As part of the

"Fast Track to Freedom" program, this approach not only enhances your technical skills but also opens up diverse revenue streams that contribute to your financial goals.

Financial Budget plan:

Chapter 6: Freelancing in the AI Era

Finding Lucrative Freelance Opportunities in AI and Tech

The rapid expansion of AI and technology has created a wealth of free-lance opportunities. Freelancers with skills in these areas are highly sought after due to their ability to drive innovation and provide competitive advantages. Here's how to find lucrative freelance jobs in AI and tech:

Identifying Your Niche

- **Specialization**: Identify specific areas within AI and tech where you excel or are most interested. This could include machine learning, natural language processing, data analysis, or software development.
- **Certifications and Education**: Enhance your credibility by obtaining certifications in tools like TensorFlow, PyTorch, AWS, or Azure. These credentials make you more attractive to potential clients.

Using Freelance Platforms

- **General Platforms**: Websites like Upwork, Freelancer, and Fiverr offer a broad range of freelance opportunities, including many in AI and tech.
- **Specialized Tech Platforms**: Toptal, Gun.io, and Gigster cater specifically to freelance tech professionals and typically offer higher-paying projects.
- **Project Bidding**: Actively bid on projects that match your skills. Tailor each proposal to the client's specific needs and highlight your unique qualifications.

Networking

- **Professional Networking Sites**: LinkedIn is invaluable. Regularly update your profile with your latest projects and skills, and engage with AI and tech groups.

- **Conferences and Workshops**: Attend industry conferences like the AI Summit or tech meetups in your area to meet potential clients and learn about new developments in the field.

Tips for Marketing Tech Skills

Marketing yourself effectively is crucial in freelancing, particularly in a high-skill, competitive field like AI. Here are strategies to enhance your visibility and appeal to potential clients:

Building a Strong Online Presence

- **Professional Website**: Create a professional website showcasing your portfolio, services, testimonials, and a blog with insights into AI topics you're knowledgeable about.
- **Social Media**: Utilize platforms like Twitter, Instagram, and Facebook to share your projects, achievements, and thoughts on AI developments.

Content Marketing

- **Blogging**: Write articles or blog posts that demonstrate your expertise and insights into AI. Share these on your social media channels and professional forums.
- **Webinars and Tutorials**: Host webinars or create tutorials on topics like starting with machine learning or using specific AI tools. These can establish you as an expert in the field.

Testimonials and Referrals

- **Client Feedback**: After completing a project, ask satisfied clients for testimonials that you can post on your website and social profiles.
- **Referral Program**: Offer incentives for clients or colleagues who refer new business to you.

Strategic Proposals

- **Custom Proposals**: Tailor each proposal to the specific project. Highlight how your specific skills can solve the client's problem or enhance their project.
- **Value Proposition**: Always articulate the tangible benefits the client will receive from your services, such as increased efficiency, reduced costs, or enhanced data insights.

Continuous Learning

- **Stay Updated**: The field of AI is rapidly evolving. Continuously update your skills and knowledge to stay relevant. Subscribe to AI newsletters, follow leading AI researchers, and participate in forums.
- **Online Courses**: Regularly engage in online courses to learn new technologies and methodologies in AI. Platforms like Coursera, edX, and MIT OpenCourseWare are great resources.

Conclusion

Freelancing in the AI era offers significant opportunities for those prepared to hone their skills and effectively market themselves. By identifying your niche, leveraging the right platforms, and using savvy marketing strategies, you can build a successful freelance career in one of the most exciting and dynamic fields today. This chapter not only equips you with the tools to find and secure freelance gigs but also helps you position yourself as a top-tier tech professional, accelerating your path to financial independence as part of the "Fast Track to Freedom" program.

Chapter 7: Writing and Publishing Profitably

Using AI to Speed Up the Writing and Editing Process

In today's digital age, AI tools have become invaluable for writers looking to enhance their productivity and improve the quality of their work. These tools can help automate mundane aspects of writing and editing, allowing authors to focus more on creative aspects.

AI in Writing

- **Content Generation**: AI writing assistants like Jasper or Sudowrite can help generate ideas, suggest content, and even draft sections of text, speeding up the writing process.
- **Language Enhancement**: Tools such as Grammarly or Hemingway use AI to improve grammar, style, and clarity, making the editing process more efficient and effective.

AI in Editing

- **Consistency Checks**: AI tools can scan a manuscript for consistency in facts, plot points, and character details, helping to maintain continuity throughout a book.
- **Feedback Generation**: AI-driven platforms can provide immediate feedback on writing style, readability, and engagement, which is especially useful for early drafts.

Self-Publishing eBooks and Print on Demand

Self-publishing has democratized the process of publishing, allowing authors to retain control over their work, from writing and design to marketing and sales.

eBooks

- **Flexibility and Reach**: eBooks provide a quick, cost-effective way to reach a global audience without the need for physical distribution.

- **Platforms**: Amazon Kindle Direct Publishing (KDP) is one of the most popular platforms for eBook publishing. It offers authors up to 70% in royalties and distributes to a vast global audience.

Print on Demand

- **No Inventory Needed**: Print on demand (POD) services allow you to sell physical books without the need to invest in inventory. Books are printed only when they are ordered, reducing risk.
- **Integration**: Services like Amazon's CreateSpace and Ingram-Spark offer seamless integration for selling print versions alongside eBooks.

Self-Publishing vs. Traditional Publishing

Advantages of Self-Publishing

- **Higher Royalties**: Self-publishing often results in higher royalties per book compared to traditional publishing.
- **Complete Creative Control**: Authors retain all creative rights and make all decisions about content, cover design, and marketing.
- **Faster Time to Market**: Self-publishing significantly reduces the time it takes for a book to reach the market.

Advantages of Traditional Publishing

- **Professional Editing and Design**: Traditional publishers provide professional services that can significantly enhance the quality of a book.
- **Distribution Networks**: Traditional publishers have established relationships with retailers and can ensure wider physical distribution.
- **Marketing and Publicity**: Publishers often have dedicated marketing teams to promote books, which can be especially beneficial for new authors.

Recommended Self-Publishing Sites

- **Amazon Kindle Direct Publishing (KDP)**: Offers easy eBook publishing with a wide reach and also includes options for print on demand via KDP Print.
- **IngramSpark**: Ideal for authors who want to maximize their book's availability as it provides extensive distribution channels including libraries and bookstores.
- **Smashwords**: A popular choice for eBooks, distributing to major retailers such as Apple iBooks, Barnes & Noble, and Kobo.

Conclusion

Writing and publishing profitably in the modern era means leveraging technology to maximize efficiency and effectiveness throughout the writing process. AI can greatly assist in both writing and editing, while self-publishing offers a viable path for maintaining control over your work and increasing potential profits. By understanding the pros and cons of self-publishing versus traditional publishing and utilizing platforms like KDP and IngramSpark, authors can navigate the publishing landscape more successfully, turning their writing efforts into profitable ventures. This chapter equips aspiring authors with the knowledge to use AI to their advantage and choose the best publishing route to meet their personal and financial goals.

Chapter 8: E-commerce and Dropshipping

Starting an Online Store with the Help of AI for Market Analysis

In the digital age, e-commerce and dropshipping have become popular avenues for entrepreneurs seeking to enter the retail market with relatively low overhead. AI can play a pivotal role in the initial stages, particularly in market analysis, to ensure that your venture starts on a strong footing.

Understanding Market Demand

Before launching an online store, it's crucial to understand the market demand. AI tools can analyze vast amounts of data from various sources to identify trends, consumer preferences, and potential niches.

- **AI-Driven Market Research**: Use AI tools like Crayon or MarketMuse that scan the internet to gather data on consumer trends, competitor strategies, and market demands. This information helps in making data-driven decisions about which products to sell, pricing strategies, and identifying gaps in the market.

Competitor Analysis

AI can automate the process of competitor analysis, providing insights into their product offerings, pricing models, marketing strategies, and customer reviews.

- **Competitive Intelligence Tools**: Tools such as Semrush and Ahrefs use AI to track competitor SEO strategies, ad spending, and website traffic. Understanding these can help you carve out a competitive edge for your store.

Product Selection

Choosing the right products is vital for the success of an online store, especially in dropshipping where inventory costs are not a burden but product relevance is critical.

- **Predictive Analytics**: Utilize predictive analytics to forecast which products are likely to perform well based on historical sales data and current market trends.

Automating Store Management with AI Tools

Once your online store is up and running, managing it efficiently becomes the next challenge. AI can automate various aspects of store management, from inventory management to customer service.

Inventory and Supplier Management

In dropshipping, managing the supply chain effectively is essential to ensure that customers receive their products promptly and in good condition.

- **AI for Inventory Management**: Tools like Linnworks and Zoho Inventory use AI to automate order processing and track stock levels across suppliers, minimizing the risks of backorders and overstock.

Dynamic Pricing

AI can dynamically adjust your product pricing based on various factors such as demand, competitor pricing, and market conditions to maximize profits.

- **Pricing Optimization Tools**: Tools such as Prisync and Competera adjust your pricing in real-time, ensuring that your store remains competitive without eroding profit margins.

Customer Service Automation

Providing excellent customer service is crucial for the success of any online store. AI can help in managing large volumes of customer interactions without compromising the quality of service.

- **Chatbots and Virtual Assistants**: Implement AI-driven chatbots like Chatfuel or Drift to handle customer inquiries, provide product recommendations, and resolve common issues around the clock.

Marketing and Customer Retention

AI can not only attract new customers but also help in retaining them by personalizing the shopping experience.

- **Email Marketing Automation**: Use tools like Mailchimp or Klaviyo that employ AI to personalize email campaigns based on customer behavior, increasing engagement and repeat purchases.
- **AI-Driven Remarketing**: Platforms like AdRoll use AI to analyze customer behavior and create personalized ad campaigns that target users who have shown interest in your products but have not completed a purchase.

Conclusion

E-commerce and dropshipping are accessible paths to entrepreneurship that can be significantly optimized with AI. From conducting thorough market analysis to automating day-to-day operations and enhancing customer interactions, AI tools can drive efficiency, reduce costs, and increase profitability. This chapter has outlined how to effectively leverage AI from the inception of your online store to its ongoing management, ensuring that your e-commerce venture is well-positioned for success in a competitive marketplace. As part of the "Fast Track to Freedom" program, these strategies are integral in using modern technology to achieve financial independence through online business operations.

Chapter 9: Investing in Stocks and Crypto with AI Assistance

AI Platforms for Predictive Market Analysis

The rapid evolution of AI technology has transformed the investment landscape by providing tools that offer predictive market analysis, helping investors make more informed decisions. In both the stock and cryptocurrency markets, these platforms help identify trends, patterns, and potential investment opportunities.

AI in Stock Market Analysis

- **Predictive Algorithms**: AI platforms like AlphaSense and Kavout use predictive algorithms to analyze historical data, identify emerging market trends, and forecast potential price movements. This data is crucial for investors looking to make strategic decisions on stock investments.
- **Natural Language Processing (NLP)**: NLP algorithms can analyze news, social media posts, and financial reports to gauge market sentiment. Sentiment analysis tools like Acuity Trading and MarketPsych can detect shifts in market mood, which often precede significant price changes.
- **Technical Analysis**: AI tools can also perform advanced technical analysis by identifying patterns in stock charts, such as head-and-shoulders or double-top formations, and detecting abnormal price movements to alert traders of potential buy or sell signals.

AI in Cryptocurrency Market Analysis

The cryptocurrency market is notoriously volatile, but AI can bring a level of predictability to the chaos.

- **Automated Market Analysis**: Platforms like Santiment and CryptoHawk use AI to analyze market data and offer trading signals, alerts, and forecasts for cryptocurrencies.
- **Sentiment Analysis**: Since crypto prices can be heavily influenced by social media sentiment, platforms like LunarCrush leverage AI

to analyze data from Twitter, Reddit, and other forums, providing investors with valuable insights into market sentiment.

- **Bot Trading**: Trading bots like CryptoHero and TradeSanta automate cryptocurrency trading strategies based on predefined rules and market trends, reducing emotional bias and allowing for more efficient trading.

Smart Investing with Robo-Advisors

Robo-advisors leverage AI and machine learning to provide automated, personalized investment management. They offer diversified portfolios and automatically rebalance them based on an investor's risk tolerance and goals.

How Robo-Advisors Work

- **Initial Assessment**: Investors start by answering a series of questions about their financial goals, risk tolerance, investment horizon, and income.
- **Portfolio Allocation**: Based on this information, the robo-advisor assigns the investor a diversified portfolio composed of low-cost exchange-traded funds (ETFs) or mutual funds, often following modern portfolio theory principles.
- **Automatic Rebalancing**: As markets fluctuate and the investor's goals evolve, the robo-advisor automatically rebalances the portfolio to maintain optimal allocation.

Popular Robo-Advisors

- **Betterment**: Offers goal-based investing and tax-efficient strategies. Betterment uses AI to allocate funds across a diversified set of ETFs and manages portfolios based on changing market conditions.
- **Wealthfront**: Provides automated portfolio management and offers a range of features like tax-loss harvesting and risk-parity strategies, all managed by AI.
- **Ellevest**: Tailored to women investors, Ellevest uses proprietary

algorithms to consider factors like gender-specific salary arcs and longer life spans in its financial planning.

Hybrid Models

Some firms combine human financial advisors with robo-advisors to provide a more comprehensive experience.

- **Schwab Intelligent Portfolios Premium**: Blends automated investing with access to human advisors, offering clients personalized financial planning and goal-setting services.
- **Vanguard Personal Advisor Services**: Combines AI-driven investment strategies with human advisors who can offer personalized advice on complex financial needs.

Conclusion

AI has emerged as a transformative force in the investment world, offering powerful predictive analytics, sentiment analysis, and automated investment management tools. Whether navigating the stock market or the volatile world of cryptocurrencies, these tools provide critical insights and automated strategies that can enhance an investor's portfolio. Robo-advisors also make investing accessible to a wider audience by offering low-cost, personalized, and efficient portfolio management. As outlined in this chapter, integrating AI into your investment strategy is a crucial component of the "Fast Track to Freedom" program, empowering investors to make data-driven decisions that can accelerate their journey toward financial independence.

Chapter 10: Building and Monetizing a YouTube Channel

Using Video Editing and Content Generation AI

Building a successful YouTube channel requires consistency, quality content, and strategic growth tactics. AI tools can streamline the process by helping with video editing and content creation, making your workflow more efficient and your videos more engaging.

AI for Video Editing

- **Automated Editing**: Tools like Magisto and Lumen5 use AI to automatically edit videos by combining video clips, music, and text overlays. They identify key moments in your footage and generate polished videos tailored to your audience.

- **Content Summarization**: Descript provides audio and video transcription, allowing creators to search their recordings for specific keywords and create concise highlights that can be used for teasers or social media snippets.

- **Visual Enhancements**: Runway ML and Adobe's Sensei AI offer features like automated background removal, color grading, and video stabilization. These tools can improve the quality of your content with minimal manual effort.

AI for Content Generation

- **Script Writing**: GPT-3-based writing assistants like Jasper can help with writing video scripts, generating ideas, and outlining content structures that keep viewers engaged.

- **Voiceover Creation**: AI voice generators like Murf or Synthesia can produce natural-sounding voiceovers, allowing you to create multilingual content or add voiceovers to existing footage quickly.
- **Thumbnail Generation**: Platforms like Canva or Snappa offer AI-driven templates that can create eye-catching video thumbnails, which are crucial for attracting clicks.

Strategies for Growing and Monetizing Viewership

Growing Viewership

- **Optimize Metadata**: Use AI tools like TubeBuddy or VidIQ to identify the best keywords, tags, and descriptions for your videos. Optimizing your metadata ensures your content ranks higher in YouTube searches.
- **Engaging Thumbnails**: Design compelling thumbnails that reflect the video's theme. Using contrasting colors, clear text, and familiar faces can significantly increase click-through rates.
- **Content Calendar**: Develop a consistent content schedule using social media management tools like Hootsuite or Buffer. Regularly posting videos helps retain subscribers and attract new viewers.
- **Collaborations**: Partner with other creators in your niche to cross-promote your channels. Collaborative videos expose your content to new audiences and often yield higher engagement.

Monetizing Viewership

- **YouTube Partner Program**: Once your channel meets the requirements (1,000 subscribers and 4,000 watch hours in the past 12 months), you can monetize through ads. Enable all ad formats, such as skippable, non-skippable, and mid-roll, to diversify revenue streams.
- **Channel Memberships and Super Chat**: Offer exclusive content,

badges, and perks to paying members. During live streams, use Super Chat to allow viewers to pay to highlight their messages.

- **Sponsorships**: Brands often collaborate with creators who cater to their target audience. Reach out to relevant companies for sponsorships, showcasing your audience demographics and engagement stats.
- **Affiliate Marketing**: Promote products you believe in and include affiliate links in video descriptions. Every time a viewer makes a purchase through your link, you earn a commission.
- **Merchandise**: Use print-on-demand services like Teespring or Spreadshop to sell branded merchandise directly from your YouTube channel, strengthening your community while creating a new income source.

Conclusion

Building and monetizing a YouTube channel is a powerful way to achieve financial freedom. By leveraging AI tools for video editing and content generation, creators can streamline their workflows and produce engaging content consistently. Moreover, strategic growth tactics such as optimizing metadata, creating eye-catching thumbnails, and collaborating with other creators can significantly expand your viewership. Monetizing through ads, sponsorships, affiliate marketing, and merchandise offers diversified revenue streams that can help sustain and grow your channel. As part of the "Fast Track to Freedom" program, this chapter provides actionable strategies that can empower you to transform your YouTube passion into a profitable business.

Chapter 11: Real Estate Income

AI Tools for Market Research and Property Management

The real estate industry has been transformed by AI, making market research and property management more data-driven, predictive, and efficient. Whether you're aiming for rental income or flipping properties, leveraging AI can enhance decision-making and profitability.

Market Research

- **Predictive Analytics**: AI tools can analyze large datasets to forecast market trends and identify emerging neighborhoods. For instance, Zillow's Zestimate uses machine learning to estimate property values, providing investors with valuable data on current and future market prices.

- **Comparative Market Analysis**: Tools like HouseCanary and CoreLogic integrate big data and machine learning to generate comparative market analysis reports, helping investors identify undervalued properties with strong growth potential.

- **Rental Yield Prediction**: Tools such as Mashvisor and AirDNA predict rental yield by analyzing local short-term and long-term rental data. They offer heat maps showing the most profitable neighborhoods for rental properties.

Property Management

- **Tenant Screening**: Automated tenant screening platforms like SmartMove and RentPrep use AI to evaluate potential tenants based on credit scores, eviction history, and employment data, ensuring a better fit and reducing tenant turnover.

- **Maintenance Automation**: Platforms like AppFolio and Buildium streamline maintenance requests using AI chatbots. Tenants can submit requests via mobile apps, while predictive maintenance tools suggest proactive repairs based on historical data.

- **Smart Home Integration**: Smart home systems can improve security and efficiency. Companies like Vivint and Nest provide

AI-enhanced security, energy-saving, and automation features, increasing the property's value and attractiveness to tenants.

Strategies for Rental Income and Property Flipping

Rental Income

- **Long-Term Rentals**: Invest in properties that can be rented out long-term, focusing on areas with strong job growth, good schools, and transportation access. Diversify your portfolio across different property types and neighborhoods to reduce risk.

- **Short-Term Rentals**: Platforms like Airbnb or Vrbo allow property owners to rent to tourists. Short-term rentals can yield higher returns but require more frequent management. Use AI tools like Beyond Pricing to optimize daily rates based on demand.

- **Real Estate Syndication**: Pool resources with other investors to purchase larger properties. As a passive investor, you receive returns proportional to your investment while benefiting from the syndicator's expertise.

- **REITs and Crowdfunding**: Invest in real estate investment trusts (REITs) or through crowdfunding platforms like Fundrise to gain exposure to rental income without directly owning property.

Property Flipping

- **Research and Acquisition**: Use AI-driven market research to identify undervalued properties in areas with high potential for appreciation. Tools like PropertyRadar provide data on foreclosures, auctions, and other distressed sales.

- **Renovation and Cost Estimation**: Estimating renovation costs is critical. AI platforms like FlipperForce help project managers accurately estimate material costs, labor expenses, and potential returns.

- **Marketing and Selling**: Utilize virtual staging tools and AI-enhanced marketing platforms to showcase the renovated property.

AI-powered marketing platforms like Adwerx and Propertybase can target specific demographics more effectively.

- **Exit Strategy**: Plan an exit strategy that minimizes holding costs. In a hot market, consider selling immediately after renovations. In a slower market, you might rent the property for a few years before selling.

Conclusion

Real estate remains a lucrative avenue for financial freedom. By utilizing AI tools for market research and property management, investors can make more informed decisions, ensuring they acquire the right properties and manage them efficiently. Rental income strategies provide steady cash flow, while property flipping offers potentially high, one-time returns. The strategies outlined in this chapter will empower you to harness the power of AI and make real estate a key component of your financial independence journey in the "Fast Track to Freedom" program.

Chapter 12: The Art of Social Media Monetization

AI Tools for Content Creation and Scheduling

In today's social media-driven world, content creation and scheduling are essential for building a profitable online presence. AI tools can streamline these tasks, enabling you to consistently deliver high-quality content that engages your audience and drives revenue.

Content Creation

- **Automated Graphics and Design**: Tools like Canva and Crello use AI-driven templates and design suggestions to help non-designers create visually appealing posts. Their extensive libraries of templates and assets can be customized to fit your brand.

- **Video Editing and Enhancement**: Tools like InVideo and Magisto employ AI to automate video editing, helping you create engaging videos with minimal effort. They can add transitions, music, and text overlays based on the context of your footage.

- **Content Generation and Copywriting**: AI writing assistants like Copy.ai or Jasper can generate compelling captions, blog posts, and ads. They analyze keywords and topics relevant to your niche to craft copy that resonates with your audience.

Scheduling and Distribution

- **Scheduling Automation**: Tools like Buffer and Hootsuite automate post scheduling, ensuring your content goes live at optimal times across multiple platforms. They offer AI-driven insights on the best posting times based on your audience's engagement patterns.

- **Content Recycling**: Platforms like MeetEdgar or SocialBee recycle evergreen content by resharing posts periodically. This allows you to maximize reach and maintain a steady stream of posts without creating new content from scratch.

- **Content Curation**: Tools like Curata and BuzzSumo analyze trending topics and recommend curated content that you can share to keep your feed fresh and relevant.

Monetizing Strategies for Different Platforms

Instagram

- **Sponsored Posts**: Brands are willing to pay for access to your audience if you have a strong following. Craft visually appealing sponsored posts, tagging the brand and using relevant hashtags.

- **Affiliate Marketing**: Share products through affiliate links in your bio or Stories. When your followers purchase through these links, you earn a commission.

- **Merchandise and Digital Products**: Use Instagram Shopping or third-party services like Shopify to sell your branded merchandise or digital products directly through the platform.

YouTube

- **Ad Revenue**: Join the YouTube Partner Program to monetize your videos with ads. Experiment with different ad formats, including skippable and non-skippable ads.

- **Channel Memberships**: Offer exclusive perks to subscribers who pay a monthly fee. Perks may include early access to videos, members-only live streams, or behind-the-scenes content.

- **Super Chat**: During live streams, enable Super Chat so viewers can pay to highlight their comments. This feature works well for channels with strong community engagement.

TikTok

- **Brand Collaborations**: Brands often partner with TikTok influencers for sponsored posts. Create short, engaging videos that align with the brand's marketing goals.
- **Creator Fund**: TikTok's Creator Fund rewards users for generating popular content. Grow your following and engagement to earn more from this fund.
- **Live Gifting**: During live streams, viewers can send virtual gifts purchased with real money. Gifts can be converted into cash through the platform.

Twitter

- **Sponsored Tweets**: Partner with brands to create sponsored tweets. These are typically short promotional messages that fit seamlessly into your feed.
- **Affiliate Links**: Share affiliate links to products relevant to your audience. Shorten links using URL shorteners like Bitly to track performance.
- **Subscription Features**: Twitter's Super Follows allows creators to offer exclusive tweets and content to paying subscribers, similar to a membership.

Facebook

- **Ad Breaks**: If you have an established audience, monetize longer videos through Facebook Ad Breaks, which inserts ads in the middle of your content.
- **Fan Subscriptions**: Offer subscription-based content, where your most dedicated fans receive exclusive posts, badges, and other perks.
- **Groups and Communities**: Create private groups that require a

subscription or fee. This is ideal for offering courses, advice, or exclusive insights.

Pinterest

- **Promoted Pins**: Collaborate with brands to create Promoted Pins. They appear in targeted users' feeds, giving products or services more visibility.
- **Affiliate Marketing**: Share affiliate links directly in pins or descriptions. Pinterest allows clickable affiliate links, making it a lucrative platform.
- **Product Pins**: If you have a Shopify store, use Rich Pins to list your products directly on Pinterest, driving traffic back to your store.

Conclusion

Social media monetization offers diverse opportunities for earning income across multiple platforms. With AI tools for content creation, scheduling, and distribution, you can maintain an engaging social media presence that attracts a loyal audience. Sponsored posts, affiliate marketing, and paid memberships provide lucrative revenue streams, allowing creators to monetize their passion projects. By understanding platform-specific strategies, you can tailor your approach for maximum profitability, ensuring social media becomes a key component in your "Fast Track to Freedom" journey toward financial independence.

Part III: Building and Managing Assets

Chapter 13: Asset Accumulation Strategies

Understanding What Assets to Build and How

Asset accumulation is a fundamental part of financial independence. By acquiring and managing various income-generating assets, you can create multiple revenue streams that help secure your financial future.

Types of Assets to Build

- **Stocks and Bonds**: Equities (stocks) and fixed-income securities (bonds) are the backbone of any diversified investment portfolio. Stocks provide growth potential, while bonds offer more stability. Consider index funds or exchange-traded funds (ETFs) for broad exposure.

- **Real Estate**: Rental properties, commercial real estate, and real estate investment trusts (REITs) are popular choices for consistent cash flow and potential appreciation.

- **Businesses and Franchises**: Acquiring or starting a small business or franchise can provide direct control over your income. Choose industries where you have expertise or a market need is evident.

- **Intellectual Property**: Earning royalties through intellectual property like patents, copyrights, and trademarks can yield passive income. Examples include writing books, creating digital products, or licensing original artwork.

- **Precious Metals**: Gold and silver have historically served as hedges against inflation and economic instability. Invest through physical bullion or exchange-traded commodities.
- **Cryptocurrency**: Despite its volatility, cryptocurrency is gaining popularity as a high-risk, high-reward asset class. Diversify across established coins and emerging tokens to manage risk.
- **Alternative Investments**: Art, collectibles, wine, or farmland can diversify your portfolio while offering unique returns.

How to Build and Manage Assets

- **Diversification**: Diversifying your assets across different classes reduces risk. Allocate assets based on your risk tolerance, investment goals, and timeline.
- **Consistent Contributions**: Make regular investments to dollar-cost average into your assets. This approach smooths out the effects of market volatility over time.
- **Compound Growth**: Reinvest dividends and interest earned on investments to compound growth over the years, increasing your net worth.
- **Leverage**: Use debt strategically to acquire appreciating assets. For instance, a mortgage can allow you to purchase rental properties and generate rental income.
- **Risk Management**: Protect your assets through insurance, emergency funds, and proper legal structures, such as trusts or LLCs.

Leveraging AI for Asset Management

Portfolio Management

- **Robo-Advisors**: Automated investment platforms like Betterment, Wealthfront, and M1 Finance offer customized, low-cost portfolios managed by AI algorithms. They automatically rebalance portfolios based on market changes and personal goals.

- **Tax Optimization**: AI tools can identify opportunities for tax-loss harvesting, which involves selling securities at a loss to offset gains elsewhere. This strategy helps minimize your tax burden.
- **Personalized Advice**: Machine learning algorithms analyze your investment history and financial goals to provide tailored advice. Platforms like Personal Capital and SigFig deliver real-time recommendations.

Real Estate Management

- **Predictive Analytics**: Machine learning models predict rental yields, property appreciation, and market trends. Platforms like Mashvisor and Reonomy use data-driven insights to help you choose profitable investment properties.
- **Automated Valuation Models (AVMs)**: Zillow's Zestimate and Redfin Estimate use AI to calculate accurate property valuations based on local market trends, recent sales, and property characteristics.
- **Tenant Screening**: Property management platforms use AI algorithms to screen tenants by analyzing financial history, credit scores, and rental records. This ensures a reliable rental income stream.

Business and Intellectual Property

- **Business Analytics**: AI-driven business analytics tools like IBM Watson Analytics and Tableau provide insights into customer behavior, market trends, and operational efficiency, helping you identify profitable opportunities.
- **IP Protection**: AI tools can monitor the web for unauthorized use of your intellectual property. Services like Red Points help detect counterfeits and infringement across marketplaces.

Cryptocurrency and Alternative Assets

- **Trading Bots**: Crypto trading bots like 3Commas and Shrimpy execute trades automatically based on market trends. They reduce emotional bias and enable efficient arbitrage across exchanges.

- **Art Valuation:** Platforms like Artnome and Artprice use machine learning to estimate the value of artworks based on historical sales data, helping collectors identify investment opportunities.

Conclusion

Asset accumulation is the cornerstone of financial independence, but building and managing assets requires strategic planning and informed decision-making. By diversifying your assets across stocks, real estate, businesses, and more, you create multiple revenue streams that safeguard your future. Leveraging AI for portfolio management, property analysis, business insights, and IP protection helps you optimize your investments, making asset management more efficient and data-driven. This chapter's strategies will enable you to utilize assets effectively on your "Fast Track to Freedom," ensuring that AI and agile hustles support your path to financial success.

Chapter 14: Intellectual Property as an Asset

Creating and Protecting Intellectual Property

Intellectual property (IP) is a valuable and often underappreciated asset in the pursuit of financial freedom. By creating and protecting your ideas, inventions, and creative works, you can generate significant passive income streams.

Types of Intellectual Property

- **Patents:** Protect inventions, whether it's a new product, process, or improvement of existing technology. Patents give exclusive rights to manufacture, use, and sell the invention for up to 20 years.
- **Trademarks:** Distinguish brands, products, or services through unique logos, slogans, or names. A registered trademark provides legal protection against infringement.
- **Copyrights:** Safeguard original literary, artistic, and musical works. This includes books, software, paintings, music, and architectural designs.

- **Trade Secrets**: Keep proprietary information confidential, such as formulas, practices, and designs that provide a competitive edge.

Creating Intellectual Property

- **Innovative Solutions**: Identify market gaps or consumer pain points and develop innovative products or processes. A patent attorney can guide you through patenting an invention.
- **Brand Building**: Create distinctive trademarks that reflect your brand identity and resonate with your target audience. Conduct a trademark search to avoid conflicts with existing brands.
- **Creative Works**: Explore your creativity in writing, music, or visual arts. Protect your work through copyright registration or use platforms like Creative Commons to license your content.
- **Documenting Trade Secrets**: Clearly document internal processes, techniques, or formulas that differentiate your business. Create policies that enforce non-disclosure agreements (NDAs).

Protecting Intellectual Property

- **Registration**: Register your patents, trademarks, and copyrights with appropriate government bodies. This provides legal protection and enables you to take action against infringers.
- **Legal Agreements**: Draft robust NDAs, licensing agreements, and employment contracts to prevent unauthorized use of your IP. Ensure employees and partners are aware of confidentiality policies.
- **Monitoring and Enforcement**: Monitor the market for infringers using AI-based IP protection services like Red Points or Corsearch. Seek legal recourse against those who violate your IP rights.

Monetizing Intellectual Assets

Licensing and Royalties

- **Licensing Agreements**: License your patents, trademarks, or copyrighted works to other businesses. These agreements allow them to use your IP while you earn royalties or licensing fees.

- **Franchising**: Create a franchise model that allows others to operate a business using your trademarks, trade secrets, and business model. Franchisees pay initial fees and ongoing royalties.
- **Music and Publishing Rights**: Earn royalties through music streaming, book publishing, or movie rights. Platforms like Spotify, Amazon Kindle, and Audible provide global reach.

Direct Commercialization

- **Product Manufacturing**: Manufacture and sell products based on your patented inventions. Partner with third-party manufacturers to expand production.
- **Brand Expansion**: License your trademark to third parties for different product categories. This expands your brand's presence and generates revenue from licensing fees.

Digital and Online Opportunities

- **Digital Products**: Develop software, eBooks, templates, or online courses. Digital products are cost-effective to produce and can be sold through platforms like Shopify, Udemy, or Etsy.
- **Subscription Models**: Offer access to exclusive content through subscription models. Patreon and Substack enable creators to monetize blogs, videos, or podcasts.
- **NFTs**: Mint digital artwork or music as non-fungible tokens (NFTs) to sell on blockchain marketplaces. NFTs ensure royalties are paid each time the work is resold.

Conclusion

Intellectual property provides lucrative opportunities for financial growth, whether through direct commercialization or licensing agreements. Creating and protecting your patents, trademarks, copyrights, and trade secrets is vital to maintain a competitive advantage. Leveraging licensing fees, royalties, digital products, and new blockchain technologies can help you unlock the potential of your intellectual assets and turn creativity into a steady stream of income. In this chapter, we explored practical strategies that will empower you to harness IP as a key pillar in your "Fast Track to Freedom" journey.

Asset Plan:

Chapter 15: Digital Assets and Their Potential

Creating Valuable Digital Products and Services

In an increasingly digital world, the creation and distribution of valuable digital assets offer immense potential for generating passive income and accelerating financial independence. Digital assets range from eBooks to courses and software, all of which can be monetized effectively.

Identifying High-Demand Digital Assets

- **EBooks and Guides**: Craft comprehensive guides or eBooks that cater to a niche audience. Popular topics include personal development, business, hobbies, and technical skills. An authoritative guide that solves a problem or shares expertise can generate consistent sales.
- **Online Courses**: Develop in-depth online courses focusing on technical skills, creative arts, or professional development. Courses that provide practical, marketable skills (e.g., coding, graphic design, digital marketing) are highly valuable.
- **Membership Sites**: Offer premium content or services through subscription-based membership sites. Members can receive exclusive content like webinars, templates, downloadable resources, and coaching sessions.
- **Templates and Tools**: Design templates, spreadsheets, or calculators that cater to specific business needs. Useful tools that save time or streamline workflows are often well-received.
- **Software and Apps**: Build software that automates repetitive tasks or enhances productivity. Even simple utility apps can find a ready market if they address a specific problem.
- **Digital Art and Music**: Artists and musicians can create and

sell digital prints, original compositions, or loops for producers. Unique digital artwork often resonates with collectors.

Developing Your Digital Product

- **Research and Planning**: Conduct market research to identify high-demand niches. Analyze competitor offerings and read reviews to find gaps and unmet needs.
- **Content Creation**: Develop high-quality, engaging content tailored to your audience. Use storytelling, case studies, and practical examples to add value.
- **Iterative Testing**: Test your product with a small audience or beta testers. Gather feedback to improve its quality and relevance.
- **Branding and Packaging**: Design professional graphics, logos, and landing pages that convey credibility. Packaging plays a significant role in customer perception.

Platforms for Selling and Trading Digital Assets

Marketplaces and Digital Distribution Platforms

- **Amazon Kindle Direct Publishing (KDP)**: Publish and sell eBooks to millions of readers on Amazon's Kindle platform. With KDP Select, authors can earn up to 70% in royalties.
- **Udemy and Teachable**: Upload and sell online courses. Udemy provides broad exposure and handles payments, while Teachable offers more control over pricing and branding.
- **Shopify**: Create your online store for digital products. Shopify's templates and plugins make it easy to set up a secure e-commerce site with payment processing.
- **Etsy**: Known for handmade and creative goods, Etsy also hosts digital downloads like printables, art prints, and eBooks.

Membership Platforms and Subscription Services

- **Patreon**: Monetize your creative work through monthly subscriptions. Offer exclusive content, early access, or personal engagement to your patrons.

- **Substack**: Publish paid newsletters to a subscription-based audience. Writers can share valuable insights, analysis, or stories with their loyal readers.

NFT Marketplaces and Blockchain Platforms

- **OpenSea**: List, buy, and sell digital art, music, and in-game items as non-fungible tokens (NFTs) on this decentralized marketplace.
- **Rarible**: Create and sell NFTs using smart contracts. Artists can set royalties that apply to future sales.
- **Foundation**: An invite-only NFT marketplace for digital artists. It provides a curated platform that emphasizes high-quality art.

Software Marketplaces and App Stores

- **Apple App Store and Google Play**: Reach billions of mobile device users by submitting apps to these widely-used app stores.
- **Gumroad**: Sell digital downloads, software, memberships, or courses. Gumroad's simple interface is ideal for independent creators.
- **CodeCanyon**: Developers can sell plugins, scripts, or themes through this marketplace, which specializes in software components.

Conclusion

Digital assets offer a broad range of opportunities for financial growth, allowing you to build scalable revenue streams that align with your skills and interests. By creating valuable digital products or services and leveraging the right platforms, you can access a global market. Whether selling eBooks, courses, software, or NFTs, tapping into this growing sector can place you on the "Fast Track to Freedom" and bring you closer to your financial independence goals.

Digital Assets plan:

Chapter 16: Traditional Assets: Stocks, Bonds, and Real Estate

Traditional assets, particularly stocks, bonds, and real estate, have long served as reliable vehicles for building wealth. With modern technology, especially artificial intelligence (AI), investors now have powerful tools to enhance portfolio management, improve decision-making, and identify emerging opportunities. This chapter explores how to optimize these traditional assets using AI-driven strategies.

Using AI for Effective Portfolio Management

Stocks

- **Stock Screening and Analysis**: AI tools like Seeking Alpha, Ziggma, and Stock Rover screen thousands of stocks to identify opportunities. Machine learning models analyze historical data, financial metrics, and market sentiment to provide actionable insights.
- **Sentiment Analysis**: AI algorithms scour news articles, social media posts, and analyst reports to gauge investor sentiment. This

analysis can inform market outlooks and identify overvalued or undervalued stocks.

- **Predictive Modeling**: Advanced AI models use historical price movements, economic indicators, and technical patterns to predict future stock prices. They can signal trends or reversals, providing investors with crucial entry and exit points.

Bonds

- **Credit Risk Analysis**: Predictive models analyze company financials, market conditions, and credit ratings to estimate the likelihood of default. Investors can gauge which bonds are too risky and which provide stable returns.
- **Yield Optimization**: AI-based portfolio optimizers create customized bond ladders, balancing yield, risk, and duration. Tools like BondView and BlackRock's Aladdin provide institutional-grade analytics.
- **Macro-Economic Analysis**: Machine learning models incorporate macroeconomic trends, such as inflation and interest rates, to assess the effect on bond yields. This analysis informs decisions about bond diversification.

Robo-Advisors

Robo-advisors offer an accessible way to leverage AI for comprehensive portfolio management. They analyze user goals, risk tolerance, and timelines to create diversified portfolios of stocks, bonds, and ETFs. Leading platforms like Betterment, Wealthfront, and SoFi automatically rebalance portfolios, harvest tax losses, and provide personalized advice.

Real Estate as a Long-Term Wealth-Building Tool

Identifying Opportunities with AI

- **Predictive Market Analytics**: AI-driven platforms like Mashvisor, Reonomy, and CoreLogic analyze property prices, rental yields, and demographic trends to forecast future appreciation and identify emerging markets.

- **Property Valuation Models**: Automated Valuation Models (AVMs) like Zillow Zestimate and Redfin Estimate use machine learning to assess home values based on comparable properties, market trends, and neighborhood data.
- **Short-Term Rental Potential**: Algorithms analyze local regulations, tourism data, and seasonal trends to determine the income potential of properties listed on Airbnb or VRBO.

Efficient Property Management

- **Tenant Screening**: Tools like RentPrep and Avail screen prospective tenants using credit scores, rental history, and employment verification. AI algorithms help identify reliable tenants, reducing vacancy rates.
- **Maintenance Optimization**: Smart property management systems predict maintenance issues and optimize energy usage. These insights minimize costly repairs and reduce operating expenses.
- **Automated Leasing**: Digital leasing platforms streamline lease agreements and renewals, collect rent electronically, and manage tenant communications.

Real Estate Financing Strategies

- **Traditional Mortgages**: Use AI-based financial calculators to evaluate the most favorable mortgage terms, considering credit score, interest rates, and down payment.
- **Real Estate Syndication**: Partner with other investors through syndication, pooling funds to purchase commercial properties. Online platforms like CrowdStreet and RealtyMogul offer access to syndicated deals.
- **REITs and Crowdfunding**: Real Estate Investment Trusts (REITs) provide exposure to diversified real estate portfolios. Crowdfunding platforms like Fundrise and DiversyFund enable small-scale investors to participate in larger projects.

Conclusion

Stocks, bonds, and real estate form the bedrock of traditional wealth-building strategies. By incorporating AI tools and data analytics into your investment approach, you gain a competitive edge in analyzing market trends, managing risk, and optimizing returns. Robo-advisors and AI platforms provide comprehensive portfolio management for stocks and bonds, while predictive analytics and automated tools streamline real estate investment. With the right strategies, these traditional assets can anchor your "Fast Track to Freedom" plan, leading you steadily toward long-term financial security.

Part IV: Diverse and Innovative Hustles

Chapter 17: Gig Economy and Micro Jobs

Identifying Profitable Gigs with AI Trend Analysis

The gig economy offers lucrative opportunities for independent contractors and freelancers to earn significant income on a flexible schedule. With the help of AI, you can identify trends and high-demand gigs that align with your skills.

AI-Driven Market Research

- **Trend Analysis**: AI algorithms analyze job postings, social media data, and freelance platforms to identify emerging trends and in-demand skills. Tools like TrendHunter and Exploding Topics uncover new niches in creative services, tech consulting, and marketing.

- **Job Aggregation**: Job boards such as Upwork, Fiverr, and Toptal use machine learning to personalize recommendations. By analyzing your skills and preferences, these platforms suggest gigs that suit your expertise and optimize your search.

- **Skill Gap Analysis**: Online learning platforms like LinkedIn Learning and Coursera use AI to identify growing skills gaps based on industry demand. This allows you to upskill or reskill in areas that offer higher-paying freelance work.

Profitable Gig Niches with AI Support

- **Content Creation and Marketing**: AI tools like Jasper and Copy.ai can generate copy, social media posts, and blog articles, reducing the time required for content creation. This is useful for marketing consultants and copywriters managing multiple clients.
- **Graphic Design and Video Editing**: Adobe Sensei, an AI platform integrated into Creative Cloud, helps designers automate repetitive tasks like background removal or content-aware fills. Video editors can use Lumen5 or InVideo to automate video creation.
- **Financial Analysis and Consulting**: Data analytics and financial modeling tools such as Power BI and Tableau help finance freelancers conduct data-driven consulting. Predictive analytics can offer insights into market trends and investment opportunities.

Profitable Gigs Without AI Assistance

- **Event Planning**: Organize weddings, corporate retreats, and social events using your networking skills and creativity. Event planning requires personal interactions and creativity that AI cannot fully replicate.
- **Handyman Services**: Basic repairs, furniture assembly, and home maintenance are in demand on platforms like TaskRabbit and Handy. Skilled labor remains essential in a range of home and commercial settings.
- **Pet Sitting and Childcare**: Services like Rover and UrbanSitter connect sitters with clients seeking personalized care. Developing a reputation for reliability and safety ensures a steady stream of referrals.
- **Driving and Delivery**: Driving with Uber or delivering food with DoorDash offers quick, consistent earnings. Though tech-driven, these jobs ultimately require human presence and judgment.

Balancing Multiple Gigs for Maximum Income

Time Management and Prioritization

- **Task Scheduling**: Use apps like Trello or Notion to schedule tasks, set reminders, and track deadlines. Prioritize high-paying or urgent tasks to maximize productivity.

- **Project Management**: Freelancers juggling multiple clients can benefit from project management software like Asana or Monday.com. These platforms help organize deliverables, track progress, and facilitate client communication.

- **Work Hours**: Establish clear work hours to avoid burnout and ensure consistent productivity. Optimize your schedule around peak productivity times and your clients' preferred working hours.

Financial Tracking

- **Invoicing and Accounting**: Use FreshBooks or QuickBooks to automate invoices and track income across multiple gigs. Set aside a portion of each payment for taxes and business expenses.

- **Budgeting Tools**: Tools like YNAB (You Need A Budget) or Mint can help allocate income for personal expenses, savings, and business investments. They provide visibility into spending patterns across various gigs.

Skill Diversification

- **Upskilling**: Continuously improve your skillset to command higher rates and access more diverse gigs. Platforms like Skillshare or edX offer a range of courses in technical, creative, and business fields.

- **Niche Specialization**: Identify complementary skills that can be packaged together for bundled services. For instance, a content writer who also knows SEO can offer a complete marketing solution.

Conclusion

The gig economy, driven by the flexibility and diversity of micro jobs, has transformed how we work and earn. By harnessing AI tools for trend analysis, time management, and skill development, you can efficiently identify and manage profitable opportunities. For gigs requiring a human touch, focus on customer satisfaction and personal branding to build lasting client relationships. With effective balance and strategic planning, this chapter can guide you through leveraging the gig economy on your "Fast Track to Freedom" path.

Chapter 18: Creating Online Courses

Online courses provide one of the most powerful ways to generate income and share expertise in the digital economy. With AI-enabled tools and sophisticated course hosting platforms, you can create high-quality educational content that resonates with your target audience. This chapter covers the process of building effective courses, leveraging AI for optimization, and selecting the best platforms for hosting and marketing.

Utilizing AI for Course Content and Structure Optimization

Topic Selection

- **Trend Identification**: Use AI tools like Google Trends, Exploding Topics, or AnswerThePublic to identify trending subjects. These tools analyze search queries and social media data to find in-demand niches.
- **Competitor Analysis**: Platforms like Udemy and Skillshare can reveal insights about competitors' courses. Tools such as Ahrefs or SEMrush help analyze the keywords and content strategies that drive traffic to these courses.

Content Creation and Enhancement

- **Research and Scripting**: AI-based content generators like Chat-GPT or Jasper can assist in drafting course scripts and lesson outlines. They generate topic ideas, answer common questions, and structure content effectively.
- **Visual Design**: AI-powered tools such as Canva and Visme provide templates, infographics, and visual elements to enrich your course. They offer intuitive designs that enhance the learning experience.
- **Video Editing**: Tools like Descript and InVideo use AI to transcribe, edit, and automate video creation. They simplify tasks like adding captions, trimming sections, or syncing audio.

Personalization and Engagement

- **Adaptive Learning**: AI-driven learning management systems (LMSs) like EdApp and LearnDash tailor courses based on individual progress and performance. Adaptive quizzes and assessments customize the learning path.
- **Gamification**: Incorporate gamified elements using AI tools like Kahoot! or Genially, which create interactive quizzes and challenges to engage learners.
- **Feedback Analysis**: Platforms like Hotjar analyze user engagement, while sentiment analysis tools provide insights from course reviews. This data informs course refinement and future marketing.

Platforms for Course Hosting and Marketing

Course Hosting Platforms

- **Udemy**: With millions of students globally, Udemy offers wide exposure for your courses. Its user-friendly platform allows you to upload videos, quizzes, and downloadable resources.
- **Teachable**: A popular platform for educators who prefer more branding control. Teachable allows you to customize course pages, pricing, and access levels.

- **Kajabi**: An all-in-one platform that combines hosting with marketing automation. Kajabi's features include email marketing, landing pages, and a robust LMS.
- **Thinkific**: Offers drag-and-drop course building and marketing features like coupons and email campaigns. Thinkific integrates with various third-party tools for analytics and payment processing.

Marketing and Promotion Strategies

- **Social Media**: Use LinkedIn, Twitter, and Facebook to promote your courses to relevant groups and networks. Share free content snippets to build credibility and drive interest.
- **Email Marketing**: Build an email list through a dedicated landing page or social media campaigns. Email newsletters are effective for announcing new courses, discounts, and free webinars.
- **Webinars and Demos**: Host live webinars to preview course content and engage directly with potential students. Platforms like Zoom or WebinarJam are ideal for these events.
- **Content Marketing**: Write blogs or record podcasts about your course topics, linking them to the course page. Content marketing establishes expertise and attracts organic traffic.

Conclusion

Creating online courses can provide a sustainable and lucrative income stream while helping others learn valuable skills. AI tools streamline content creation, improve course structure, and enhance learner engagement, giving your courses a competitive edge. Selecting the right hosting platform is crucial for branding and managing the user experience, while a well-rounded marketing strategy ensures your courses reach the right audience. Incorporating these best practices in your "Fast Track to Freedom" journey will maximize the impact and profitability of your online courses.

Chapter 19: Mobile Apps and Software Development

The mobile app and software industry has expanded significantly in recent years, opening the door to countless opportunities for developers to earn income. With AI enhancing productivity and improving quality control, it's easier than ever to identify profitable niches and create high-quality apps. This chapter explores the trends in profitable app niches and how AI can streamline development and testing.

Trends in Profitable App Niches

Market Analysis

- **Market Research Tools**: Platforms like App Annie and Sensor Tower provide insights into app download trends, user demographics, and monetization strategies. These tools reveal which niches are performing well and where gaps exist.

- **Competitor Benchmarking**: By analyzing competitor apps, you can identify features, pricing models, and user experiences that resonate with the target audience. Ahrefs and SimilarWeb offer insights into competitor traffic and marketing strategies.

Niche Opportunities

- **Fitness and Wellness Apps**: Fitness apps that offer personalized training plans or wellness tracking are in high demand. Features like AI-based coaching, habit trackers, and diet planning are especially popular.

- **Productivity and Collaboration**: Remote work trends drive demand for apps that enhance productivity and streamline collaboration. Note-taking, project management, and video conferencing apps with integrations are sought after.

- **E-commerce and Retail**: Mobile shopping apps offer personalized recommendations, AR/VR product visualization, and seamless payment options. Specialized apps for product reviews or price comparisons also see growth.
- **Educational and Learning**: EdTech apps that deliver adaptive learning, personalized study paths, and engaging gamification continue to attract users. Content tailored to different age groups and proficiency levels is a key differentiator.
- **Finance and Budgeting**: FinTech apps help users manage budgets, track expenses, and automate savings. Niche features like investment tracking, tax planning, and credit score monitoring are valuable.
- **Gaming and Entertainment**: Casual games and social media-integrated apps generate revenue through in-app purchases and ads. AR-based games and streaming services are particularly profitable.

Using AI Tools for App Development and Testing

Streamlining Development

- **Natural Language Processing (NLP)**: Tools like OpenAI's Codex and GitHub Copilot can write code based on plain-language instructions, speeding up the development process. They can suggest boilerplate code, auto-complete functions, and identify bugs.
- **Automated Frameworks**: App-building frameworks like Flutter, React Native, and Xamarin allow developers to write cross-platform code. AI tools enhance these frameworks by identifying performance bottlenecks and recommending improvements.
- **Prototyping and Design**: Platforms like Figma, Sketch, and Adobe XD use AI to predict design layouts, suggest UI elements, and automate repetitive design tasks. They can generate app wireframes and prototypes quickly.

- **Code Refactoring and Optimization**: Tools like DeepCode and SonarQube analyze codebases to detect errors, recommend improvements, and ensure consistency. Refactoring improves performance and reduces technical debt.

Efficient Testing and Quality Assurance

- **Test Case Generation**: Tools like Testim and Applitools use machine learning to generate and prioritize test cases based on past bugs and user behavior. They improve test coverage while reducing testing time.
- **Automated Regression Testing**: Selenium and Appium are widely used for automating regression tests, and AI-enhanced tools like Mabl identify UI changes that might cause test failures.
- **Performance Testing**: AI-powered tools like Neotys and Blaze-Meter simulate real-world load conditions and identify performance bottlenecks. They analyze resource usage patterns to optimize app efficiency.
- **User Feedback Analysis**: Sentiment analysis tools like Monkey-Learn and Lexalytics analyze reviews and customer feedback to identify recurring issues or desired features. They help prioritize the app's roadmap.

Conclusion

The demand for innovative mobile apps and software solutions presents an immense opportunity for developers. Understanding profitable niches ensures that your app caters to the needs of your target audience, while AI tools streamline development, testing, and user analysis. Integrating these strategies and technologies into your workflow will enhance efficiency and quality, putting you on the "Fast Track to Freedom." With the right planning and tools, you can build and monetize apps that thrive in today's digital landscape.

Chapter 20: Arts and Crafts: Turning Hobbies into Cash

Turning your passion for arts and crafts into a lucrative business is more feasible than ever with the support of technology and online platforms. By understanding market trends, using AI for optimization, and tapping into thriving e-commerce platforms, you can transform your creative skills into a profitable venture. This chapter explores how to analyze market opportunities using AI and leverage online platforms to sell handmade goods.

Market Analysis Using AI

Identifying Trends and Niches

- **Search Trends**: Tools like Google Trends or Ahrefs provide insights into search volume for specific arts and crafts-related terms. You can identify what materials, styles, and crafts are currently popular or rising in interest.
- **Social Media Analysis**: Hashtag analysis and social listening tools such as Hootsuite or Brandwatch can reveal emerging trends on Instagram, Pinterest, and TikTok, where crafting communities thrive. They help identify the types of crafts that resonate with target demographics.
- **Marketplaces and Competition**: Use e-commerce marketplaces like Etsy and Amazon Handmade to analyze top-selling items, pricing strategies, and customer preferences. Tools like Marmalead and Craftybase offer Etsy-specific analytics.

Demand Forecasting

- **Predictive Analytics**: AI platforms like SAS or RapidMiner analyze sales data, seasonal trends, and market events to forecast demand. This helps you optimize inventory and plan production schedules.
- **Product Personalization**: AI-based recommendation engines suggest customizations or complementary items based on customer

behavior. Personalization increases perceived value and drives higher conversion rates.

- **Supply Chain Management**: For artisans relying on raw materials, AI-powered inventory management systems like TradeGecko or Unleashed automate reordering and identify the best suppliers.

Online Platforms for Selling Handmade Goods

Specialized Marketplaces

- **Etsy**: The largest global marketplace for handmade goods, Etsy provides easy-to-use shop tools, extensive analytics, and advertising options. It's ideal for artisans seeking exposure to a broad, craft-focused audience.
- **Amazon Handmade**: An extension of Amazon, this marketplace offers a vast customer base and Prime benefits. Listing handmade products requires an application but gives access to Amazon's fulfillment network.
- **Aftcra**: Focused on American-made crafts, Aftcra appeals to buyers seeking unique, locally made goods. It's a curated platform that emphasizes high-quality, niche products.
- **Folksy**: A UK-based marketplace specializing in crafts and design. Ideal for artisans targeting European buyers, it promotes British creativity and craftsmanship.

General E-Commerce Platforms

- **Shopify**: A customizable platform that allows you to build a branded e-commerce website, complete with product pages, payment processing, and marketing tools. It's suitable for artisans who want to establish their own online identity.
- **WooCommerce**: An open-source WordPress plugin that turns a website into a fully functional online store. It integrates with WordPress themes, plugins, and marketing tools.
- **Big Cartel**: Popular among artists and crafters, Big Cartel offers

simple store-building tools and focuses on independent sellers with smaller inventories.

Social Media Sales Channels

- **Instagram Shop**: By enabling shopping tags, Instagram lets artisans showcase and sell products directly through their feed and stories. Collaborate with influencers or use targeted ads to boost reach.

- **Facebook Marketplace**: Enables quick and easy listing of handmade goods and appeals to a broad audience. Facebook Shop integrates with Instagram Shop for a unified selling experience.

- **Pinterest Shop**: Pinterest is a go-to platform for discovering new crafts and provides buyable pins that let users purchase directly. Pinterest Ads and Promoted Pins can drive additional traffic to your shop.

Marketing Strategies for Success

- **SEO Optimization**: Use keyword research to optimize product titles, descriptions, and tags for higher visibility in search results. Tools like Keywords Everywhere or KWFinder help identify relevant terms.

- **Content Marketing**: Create blog posts, videos, or how-to guides demonstrating your creative process or showcasing product use. Content marketing builds credibility and engages potential customers.

- **Email Marketing**: Build an email list through your website or at craft fairs. Regular newsletters with new products, promotions, and crafting tips nurture customer loyalty.

- **Influencer Collaborations**: Partner with influencers who resonate with your brand. Their followers often trust their recommendations, and collaborations can drive substantial traffic.

Conclusion

By conducting thorough market analysis using AI tools, identifying trending niches, and using the right platforms, you can turn your artistic hobbies into a sustainable business. Specialized marketplaces like Etsy and Amazon Handmade, alongside custom e-commerce platforms, offer ample opportunities for artisans to sell their products. Strategic marketing, whether through content or collaborations, ensures that your audience grows and stays engaged. Integrate these steps into your "Fast Track to Freedom" journey to transform your creativity into a rewarding financial venture.

Side gig Plan:

Chapter 21: *Financial Blogging and Influencing*

In the digital age, financial blogging and influencing have evolved into powerful income-generating ventures. With AI-driven tools, content creators can produce high-quality material while optimizing for SEO. Monetization strategies span from traditional advertising to affiliate marketing and sponsored content. This chapter will guide you through leveraging AI for content creation and effective SEO while exploring proven monetization strategies.

AI-Driven Content Creation and SEO

Content Generation and Writing

- **Topic Research and Ideas**: Tools like AnswerThePublic or BuzzSumo help identify trending questions, keywords, and topics in personal finance. AI-powered content generators like Jasper or ChatGPT generate outlines and article drafts, cutting down on research time.
- **Content Enhancement**: Grammarly and Hemingway Editor use AI to analyze grammar, clarity, and tone, ensuring that your writing style is consistent and readable. They highlight complex sentences or unnecessary jargon, creating polished articles that appeal to readers.
- **Content Repurposing**: Use tools like Lumen5 or Descript to convert blog posts into engaging videos or podcasts. This multiplies content reach across different formats and platforms.

Search Engine Optimization (SEO)

- **Keyword Optimization**: AI-based tools like Surfer SEO or SEMrush provide keyword recommendations, analyze competitor sites, and assess keyword difficulty. Incorporating these keywords helps your content rank higher on search engines.

- **Content Structure and Readability**: Yoast SEO and Clearscope analyze content for readability, internal linking, and keyword distribution. They guide the structure of headings, paragraphs, and subtopics to ensure user-friendly navigation.
- **Backlink Analysis**: Ahrefs and Moz evaluate your backlink profile and suggest potential sites for guest posting or partnership. Building strong backlinks improves your site's domain authority and search engine ranking.
- **AI-Powered Analytics**: Tools like Google Analytics or Hotjar use machine learning to analyze user behavior, traffic patterns, and conversion funnels. This data guides content adjustments and marketing strategies.

Monetization Strategies for Blogs and Social Media

Advertising

- **Display Ads**: Ad networks like Google AdSense or Mediavine place relevant ads on your blog, earning revenue based on clicks or impressions. Display ads are straightforward but require significant traffic to be highly profitable.
- **Sponsored Content**: Brands pay for sponsored blog posts or social media content that subtly promotes their products or services. Creating authentic and engaging sponsored posts increases user trust.
- **Video Monetization**: If you have a YouTube channel, Google AdSense allows video monetization. Longer videos (10+ minutes) can contain multiple ads to boost earnings.

Affiliate Marketing

- **Affiliate Networks**: Join networks like ShareASale, CJ Affiliate, or Rakuten to access a wide range of finance-related products.

These networks provide affiliate links to embed in blog posts or social media.

- **Product Reviews and Recommendations**: Write in-depth reviews of financial products like investment platforms, budgeting apps, or online banks. Authentic recommendations backed by your own usage build credibility.

- **Tutorials and Case Studies**: Create tutorials on using affiliate products or case studies on how they helped solve a problem. Educational content tends to perform well for conversions.

Premium Content and Memberships

- **eBooks and Guides**: Create comprehensive eBooks or downloadable guides focused on specific financial topics, such as investing, debt reduction, or retirement planning. Selling them directly or through platforms like Amazon Kindle creates an additional revenue stream.

- **Online Courses**: Develop courses covering various financial literacy topics. Platforms like Teachable or Udemy help market and sell these courses.

- **Membership Communities**: Offer exclusive content through subscription-based memberships. Use platforms like Patreon or Substack to deliver premium newsletters, webinars, or personalized financial advice.

Brand Collaborations and Influencer Marketing

- **Social Media Sponsorships**: Brands often sponsor posts on Instagram, TikTok, and Twitter if you have a substantial following. These collaborations are especially effective with micro-influencers who have loyal audiences.

- **Collaborative Webinars and Events**: Host co-branded webinars or live events with financial companies. These events position you as a thought leader and attract sponsorships or speaking fees.

- **Giveaways and Challenges**: Collaborate with brands to host giveaways, challenges, or promotions that generate buzz. These events increase engagement and provide valuable leads for follow-up marketing.

Conclusion

Financial blogging and influencing offer immense potential for income generation when optimized with AI-driven tools and effective monetization strategies. Content creation becomes efficient and high-quality with AI's assistance, while SEO ensures better reach and visibility. Monetization strategies like advertising, affiliate marketing, premium content, and brand collaborations provide multiple income streams. Incorporating these strategies into your "Fast Track to Freedom" journey will enable you to thrive as a financially savvy digital influencer.

Chapter 22: Subscription Services and Membership Sites

Subscription services and membership sites have become increasingly popular business models, offering creators predictable, recurring revenue streams. They are particularly well-suited to niches where exclusive, value-added content or services can be delivered regularly. AI significantly improves subscription management, content personalization, and customer retention. In this chapter, we'll delve into the setup and management of subscriptions using AI, along with strategies to engage and retain subscribers.

Setting Up and Managing Subscriptions with AI

Identifying Your Subscription Model

- **Membership Tiers:** Different tiers can offer varying levels of access and benefits, from basic content to premium consulting or products. This model provides value differentiation and appeals to diverse customer segments.

- **Monthly vs. Annual Plans**: Offering both monthly and annual plans provides flexibility. Annual plans usually have discounts to encourage longer-term commitment, while monthly plans appeal to budget-conscious subscribers.

- **Content and Service Types**: Curate your content or services based on target demographics and interests. Subscription-based digital content could include newsletters, courses, webinars, or coaching. Physical goods might consist of curated product boxes or exclusive access to events.

AI Tools for Subscription Management

- **Subscription Platforms**: Platforms like Patreon, Substack, and Memberful manage payments, access control, and analytics. They integrate with email marketing and CMS tools.

- **Automated Payment Processing**: Solutions like Stripe, Chargebee, or Recurly manage subscription billing cycles, sending automatic reminders for payment and offering multiple payment options.

- **Personalization and Recommendations**: Tools like HubSpot, Pega, and Segment analyze user behavior to deliver tailored recommendations. This personalization increases perceived value and drives higher conversion rates.

- **Churn Reduction**: AI tools like Custify and ProfitWell detect early signs of churn, such as reduced engagement or downgrades, triggering targeted retention campaigns. They can suggest discounts, survey lapsed members, or flag accounts requiring personal intervention.

- **Usage Analytics**: Google Analytics and Hotjar provide insights into subscriber engagement patterns, highlighting popular content or services. Segmenting data by subscription tiers helps optimize value for each group.

Engaging and Retaining Subscribers

Onboarding and Orientation

- **Welcome Sequence**: A welcome email sequence or onboarding guide introduces new members to the benefits of their subscription. Ensure the tone is warm and encouraging, inviting them to explore key content.
- **Exclusive Community Access**: Private forums, Slack groups, or Discord channels foster a sense of belonging. Encourage introductions and highlight member achievements to strengthen the community spirit.
- **Quick Wins**: Provide early wins through introductory content or offers, reinforcing the value of their membership and encouraging immediate engagement.

Content Strategy and Calendar

- **Regular Publishing**: Maintain a consistent publishing schedule so members anticipate new content. A content calendar ensures variety and a steady stream of releases.
- **Exclusive Content**: Offer content that isn't available publicly, like advanced tutorials, research reports, or exclusive Q&A sessions. Create a tier-specific roadmap to clarify what each membership level can expect.
- **Personalization**: Send personalized content recommendations via email or directly in their dashboard. Analyze engagement metrics to refine recommendations over time.
- **Member-Generated Content**: Encourage members to contribute questions, suggestions, or even articles. Recognition through features or rewards fosters loyalty.

Retention Strategies

- **Surveys and Feedback**: Regularly collect feedback to understand shifting needs. Quick surveys or voting polls reveal popular content types, subscription value perception, and potential pain points.
- **Loyalty Programs and Gamification**: Reward loyal subscribers

with discounts, badges, or early access. Gamification elements like points, leaderboards, or challenges incentivize engagement.

- **Live Interactions**: Host live Q&A sessions, webinars, or expert interviews that members can participate in directly. Live interactions create urgency and a unique value proposition.
- **Automated Win-Back Campaigns**: For subscribers who cancel or lapse, create automated campaigns offering discounts, exclusive previews, or personal outreach to re-engage them.

Analytics and Continuous Improvement

- **Engagement Metrics**: Analyze time spent, content views, and click-through rates to identify engagement patterns and optimize content strategy.
- **Member Satisfaction**: Monitor satisfaction scores or direct feedback to understand the value proposition. Adjust offerings accordingly.
- **Business KPIs**: Track KPIs like customer acquisition cost, lifetime value, and churn rate. Use this data to refine marketing strategies, content offerings, and subscription tiers.

Conclusion

Subscription services and membership sites, when set up and managed well, can generate sustainable, recurring revenue while delivering exceptional value to subscribers. By leveraging AI for management, personalization, and churn reduction, you can ensure the growth and stability of your membership base. Developing a clear onboarding strategy, consistent content calendar, and data-driven retention tactics will help engage and retain subscribers. With these practices in your "Fast Track to Freedom," you'll build a membership model that thrives over time.

Part V: Advanced Financial Strategies and Scaling

Chapter 23: Advanced Tax Strategies and Efficiency

Tax planning is essential for maximizing profitability and ensuring compliance. For business owners and individuals aiming to achieve financial independence, understanding advanced tax strategies and leveraging AI tools is crucial. This chapter explores how AI can help optimize taxes, track expenses, and employ legal strategies to minimize tax liabilities.

Using AI for Tax Optimization and Tracking Expenses

AI-Driven Tax Optimization

- **Income Structuring**: AI-powered platforms like TurboTax, QuickBooks, and TaxJar analyze your income sources, business expenses, and financial history to identify potential deductions and credits. They suggest optimal ways to structure income, such as recharacterizing dividends or deferring bonuses, to minimize taxes.

- **Retirement Accounts**: AI tools analyze your retirement contributions and recommend adjusting the mix of taxable and nontaxable accounts. They may suggest converting traditional IRAs to Roth IRAs during low-income years or maximizing 401(k) contributions.

- **Deductions and Credits**: Automated tax preparation software identifies deductions and credits, often overlooked manually. These include energy-efficient home credits, educational credits, and deductions for charitable contributions or health savings accounts.

- **Tax-Loss Harvesting**: Robo-advisors like Betterment or Wealthfront automatically execute tax-loss harvesting, selling losing investments to offset gains. The AI continuously monitors portfolios to identify opportunities for maximizing after-tax returns.

Tracking Expenses with AI

- **Expense Categorization**: AI software such as Expensify or Zoho Expense categorizes business expenses automatically by analyzing receipts and transactions. They identify which expenses are deductible and highlight unusual spending patterns.
- **Receipt Management**: Apps like Dext and Shoeboxed allow users to scan receipts and bills. They use OCR (Optical Character Recognition) technology to extract and organize relevant data for tax purposes.
- **Mileage Tracking**: For those using vehicles for business, mileage tracking apps like MileIQ and Hurdlr automatically track distance and log mileage for IRS-compliant deductions.
- **AI-Enhanced Bookkeeping**: QuickBooks Online, Xero, and FreshBooks use AI to automate bookkeeping, reducing errors and ensuring consistent classification. They synchronize with bank accounts, credit cards, and payment processors.
- **Predictive Tax Calculations**: Some platforms offer predictive tax calculations based on historical trends, current year projections, and potential tax law changes. This insight helps preempt cash flow issues.

Legal Strategies to Minimize Tax Liabilities

Business Structuring

- **Entity Selection**: For entrepreneurs, the right business structure (LLC, S-Corp, C-Corp, or partnership) determines tax treatment.

An S-Corp may allow owners to save on self-employment taxes by splitting income into salary and dividends.

- **Qualified Business Income (QBI) Deduction**: Under the Tax Cuts and Jobs Act, many small business owners can deduct up to 20% of qualified business income. Ensuring your business meets the requirements and correctly claiming this deduction can significantly lower tax liability.

- **Income Splitting**: Shifting income to family members in lower tax brackets via legitimate wages or gifts can reduce overall tax liability. Employing a spouse or adult child in the business or funding education via 529 plans are potential methods.

Tax-Advantaged Investments

- **Retirement Plans**: Maximize contributions to employer-sponsored retirement plans like 401(k)s or solo 401(k)s. SEP-IRAs and SIMPLE IRAs offer additional opportunities for the self-employed.

- **Health Savings Accounts (HSAs)**: Contributions to HSAs are tax-deductible, and qualified medical expenses are tax-free. The account balance can grow over time, providing a valuable retirement supplement.

- **Real Estate Investments**: Real estate investors can benefit from depreciation deductions, Section 1031 exchanges, and cost segregation. These strategies defer taxes and reduce taxable rental income.

- **Opportunity Zones**: Investing in Opportunity Zones allows deferral or reduction of capital gains taxes. Holding the investment for ten years or more may eliminate gains taxes entirely.

International Tax Considerations

- **Foreign Tax Credit**: If you earn income abroad, the Foreign Tax Credit prevents double taxation by reducing your U.S. tax liability by the amount paid to foreign governments.

- **Expatriate Exclusion**: U.S. citizens living abroad can exclude up to a certain amount of foreign-earned income from taxation. The exclusion applies if you meet residency requirements.

- **Transfer Pricing**: For multinational businesses, transfer pricing ensures intra-company transactions are priced appropriately to minimize global tax liabilities while complying with international tax laws.

Conclusion

Advanced tax strategies and AI-driven tools can significantly reduce tax liabilities while ensuring compliance. Automated tax optimization identifies deductions and credits that maximize after-tax income, while AI-enhanced expense tracking simplifies record-keeping. Business structuring, tax-advantaged investments, and international tax considerations provide legal means to minimize tax burdens. Incorporate these strategies into your "Fast Track to Freedom" journey to maximize profitability and maintain financial independence.

Chapter 24: Franchising and Scaling Businesses

Expanding a business through franchising or scaling existing operations can unlock significant revenue streams. With the help of AI analysis and technology-driven processes, entrepreneurs can assess franchise opportunities effectively and scale businesses with minimal growing pains. In this chapter, we'll cover how AI aids franchise evaluation and outline the steps to efficiently scale a business using technology.

Evaluating Franchise Opportunities with AI Analysis

Market Research and Trend Analysis

- **Industry Trends**: AI-powered market research tools like Crayon and CB Insights monitor industry trends, revealing sectors with high growth potential. By analyzing macroeconomic trends, consumer behavior, and emerging technologies, these tools identify franchise industries on the rise.

- **Competitor Benchmarking**: Tools like SimilarWeb and SEMrush assess competitor performance by analyzing their traffic, marketing strategies, and customer engagement. Benchmarking helps gauge how your potential franchise would stack up in the current market.

- **Location Analysis**: Predictive analytics tools like SiteZeus and Maptive evaluate demographic data and foot traffic patterns to identify prime franchise locations. They predict local demand based on population density, income levels, and business competition.

Financial Analysis and Profit Projections

- **Revenue Modeling**: Tools like Bizminer or QuickBooks Financial Planner analyze historical revenue data to project future franchise profitability. They estimate market saturation, expected demand, and break-even timelines.
- **Franchise Disclosure Documents (FDDs)**: AI tools such as Docugami or Kira analyze FDDs to identify contractual risks and obligations. They highlight clauses related to fees, territory restrictions, and intellectual property.
- **Cash Flow Analysis**: Automated accounting platforms provide real-time cash flow analysis, ensuring that franchisees maintain the liquidity required for working capital, royalty fees, and expansion costs.
- **Risk Assessment**: Machine learning models, like those from Moody's Analytics or Experian, evaluate credit risk, supply chain vulnerabilities, and market volatility to help franchisees mitigate financial risks.

Franchise Support System

- **Training Programs**: Evaluate the franchisor's training programs through reviews, third-party audits, and online reputation analysis. Effective programs help franchisees master business operations quickly.
- **Marketing Support**: Analyze the franchisor's marketing strategy, including SEO, social media, and branding initiatives. Assess if they offer franchisees co-op advertising funds or marketing material templates.
- **Supply Chain Management**: Determine if the franchisor provides

negotiated supplier pricing and centralized procurement. Their supply chain should be agile enough to adapt to market fluctuations.

Steps to Scale a Business Efficiently with Technology

Streamlining Business Operations

- **Cloud-Based ERP Systems**: Cloud-based ERP (Enterprise Resource Planning) systems like NetSuite or Microsoft Dynamics integrate business functions like finance, HR, inventory, and sales. They provide real-time data to streamline decision-making.

- **Automation Tools**: Robotic process automation (RPA) tools like UiPath and Blue Prism automate repetitive tasks in accounting, HR, and customer support. This reduces human error and frees up staff for strategic tasks.

- **Inventory Management**: Tools like TradeGecko or Katana optimize inventory levels by analyzing sales trends and demand forecasting. They also automate reorder alerts and supplier communications.

Marketing and Customer Engagement

- **Customer Relationship Management (CRM)**: Salesforce, HubSpot, and Zoho CRM consolidate customer data, enabling targeted marketing campaigns and personalized engagement.

- **Chatbots and Virtual Assistants**: AI chatbots like Drift or Intercom handle basic customer inquiries, appointment scheduling, and lead qualification. This reduces customer support workload while providing 24/7 assistance.

- **Marketing Automation**: Platforms like Mailchimp or Marketo segment email lists, analyze user behavior, and personalize messaging. Automated drip campaigns nurture leads over time.

Workforce and Talent Management

- **AI-Powered Recruitment**: Tools like LinkedIn Recruiter and

Lever source candidates, assess resumes, and schedule interviews. AI algorithms match applicants to the most suitable roles.

- **Employee Training**: Learning management systems (LMS) like TalentLMS or Coursera for Business provide digital training modules tailored to employee roles. They track progress and identify areas for further development.
- **Performance Analytics**: Tools like Lattice or Culture Amp gather employee feedback, set goals, and track KPIs. This data-driven approach to performance management identifies productivity gaps and training needs.

Financial Management and Data Analytics

- **Budgeting and Forecasting**: Financial planning software like Adaptive Insights or Prophix enables multi-scenario budgeting and forecasting. They integrate with accounting systems for real-time cash flow visibility.
- **KPI Dashboards**: Business intelligence platforms like Tableau or Power BI visualize key performance indicators (KPIs) across departments. Dashboards help identify high-performing and under-performing areas.
- **Predictive Analytics**: AI-driven analytics tools identify sales trends, customer churn risks, and emerging market opportunities. They guide strategic decision-making for expansion.

Conclusion

Franchising and scaling are lucrative paths when evaluated and executed with the right strategies and technological support. AI analysis ensures comprehensive due diligence when assessing franchise opportunities, covering market trends, financial projections, and support systems. Meanwhile, efficient scaling hinges on streamlining operations, engaging customers, managing talent, and leveraging data analytics. Incorporating these approaches in your "Fast Track to Freedom" will pave the way for successful expansion.

Chapter 25: Wealth Management and Investment Diversification

As you aim to build and protect wealth, efficient portfolio diversification and effective risk management are key. Artificial intelligence (AI) is transforming wealth management by offering data-driven insights, enabling precise diversification strategies, and helping investors assess and manage risks. This chapter will explore how AI enhances wealth management and the ways in which technology assists with identifying and mitigating investment risks.

AI in Wealth Management for Portfolio Diversification

Personalized Portfolio Construction

- **Robo-Advisors:** Platforms like Betterment, Wealthfront, and Schwab Intelligent Portfolios analyze your financial goals, risk tolerance, and time horizon. They build customized, diversified portfolios using index funds and ETFs, automatically rebalancing them as needed.

- **Goal-Based Investing**: AI-driven tools segment financial goals into distinct buckets (e.g., retirement, education, home purchase), creating tailored sub-portfolios for each. They assign assets based on expected returns and risk tolerance to meet those specific targets.
- **Thematic Investing**: Tools like Motif or iShares Core Portfolio offer thematic ETFs and portfolios centered around long-term trends like clean energy, technology, and emerging markets. AI systems identify relevant stocks and weigh them for maximum exposure while maintaining diversification.

Advanced Asset Allocation

- **Modern Portfolio Theory**: Portfolio management platforms incorporate Harry Markowitz's Modern Portfolio Theory to optimize asset allocation. They calculate expected returns, variance, and covariance of various assets to design efficient, low-risk portfolios.
- **Alternative Asset Classes**: AI platforms recommend alternative investments like REITs, commodities, private equity, and cryptocurrencies for portfolio diversification. Their proprietary models weigh these classes for hedging against market volatility.
- **Factor-Based Investing**: AI-driven tools screen assets based on specific factors such as value, growth, momentum, and quality. They identify factor combinations that yield higher returns while minimizing correlated risks.

Automated Rebalancing

- **Risk Monitoring**: Robo-advisors continuously monitor the market and rebalance portfolios if specific risk thresholds are breached. They adjust asset classes and weights to preserve the desired risk-return profile.
- **Tax-Efficient Strategies**: Automated tools execute tax-loss harvesting, strategically selling underperforming assets to offset taxable

gains. They replace them with similar investments to maintain diversification.

- **Cash Flow Adjustments**: Rebalancing algorithms also account for new cash flows (e.g., dividends, deposits), reinvesting them in assets needing higher allocation.

Assessing and Managing Investment Risks with Technology

Comprehensive Risk Analysis

- **Value at Risk (VaR)**: Portfolio management tools calculate Value at Risk (VaR), estimating the potential loss in a portfolio over a given period. They analyze historical volatility and simulate market scenarios.
- **Monte Carlo Simulations**: These simulations project thousands of potential market outcomes based on historical data and statistical distributions. This helps assess the probability of portfolio returns falling short of specific targets.
- **Stress Testing**: Platforms perform stress tests simulating worst-case scenarios, like recessions or market crashes, to evaluate how portfolios would perform. They suggest adjustments to mitigate potential risks.
- **Sentiment Analysis**: Tools like AlphaSense and RavenPack analyze market sentiment by parsing financial news, earnings calls, and social media. They offer early warnings for potential market disruptions.

Mitigating Investment Risks

- **Portfolio Hedging**: Automated systems suggest hedging strategies using options, derivatives, or inverse ETFs to protect against downside risks. This minimizes potential losses in adverse markets.
- **Scenario-Based Asset Allocation**: AI tools analyze macroeconomic scenarios to recommend optimal asset allocation. For instance, in an inflationary scenario, they might increase exposure to commodities and inflation-protected securities.

- **Diversification Monitoring**: Regularly monitoring asset correlation helps maintain an effective diversification strategy. AI systems alert investors when portfolio correlations exceed thresholds, recommending adjustments.
- **Tail Risk Management**: Tail risk hedging strategies use AI algorithms to detect and protect against rare, high-impact events. They may include put options, long volatility funds, or derivatives.

Automated Risk Reporting

- **Performance Dashboards**: Business intelligence tools like Tableau or Power BI provide real-time dashboards with risk metrics, KPIs, and historical performance charts. They compare returns against benchmarks to highlight areas for improvement.
- **Regulatory Compliance**: AI systems ensure portfolios comply with regulatory requirements, such as diversification limits or anti-money laundering protocols.
- **Custom Reports**: Reporting tools automatically generate customized performance and risk reports for different stakeholders, helping them make data-driven investment decisions.

Conclusion

Effective wealth management requires comprehensive diversification and meticulous risk management. AI helps construct personalized portfolios, execute automated rebalancing, and manage risks with unparalleled precision. By leveraging robo-advisors, advanced asset allocation, and predictive analytics, investors can diversify across asset classes while staying resilient to market disruptions. Incorporate these practices into your "Fast Track to Freedom" to safeguard and grow your wealth strategically.

Saving Budget plan:
Goal:

Chapter 26: Navigating Financial Regulations and Compliance

Navigating the maze of financial regulations and ensuring compliance is vital for securing long-term success in any wealth-building strategy. With evolving rules, increasing scrutiny, and complex requirements, leveraging artificial intelligence (AI) to stay compliant is crucial. In this chapter, we'll explore how AI simplifies regulatory compliance and provide an overview of the legal landscape.

AI Tools for Regulatory Compliance and Updates

Regulatory Intelligence Systems

- **Global Rule Tracking**: Tools like Thomson Reuters Regulatory Intelligence and Wolters Kluwer provide real-time updates on global regulatory changes. They monitor policy developments across multiple jurisdictions and alert you to new rules affecting your business or investments.

- **Natural Language Processing (NLP)**: Compliance tools with NLP capabilities, like Ascent RegTech, interpret complex regulations to identify key obligations. They categorize obligations by sector and jurisdiction, simplifying the process of identifying relevant rules.

- **Risk Categorization**: AI models evaluate the impact of new regulations on specific business operations and investments. They classify risks into low, medium, and high categories to prioritize compliance efforts.

Compliance Automation and Monitoring

- **Automated Reporting**: Regulatory reporting platforms like AxiomSL automate the generation and submission of mandatory reports, such as Form 13F, tax filings, and anti-money laundering (AML) reports. They integrate with accounting software to minimize data discrepancies.
- **KYC and AML Compliance**: Know Your Customer (KYC) and Anti-Money Laundering (AML) platforms like ComplyAdvantage and LexisNexis Risk Solutions screen clients against sanction lists, political exposure databases, and adverse media. Machine learning models flag suspicious transactions and behavior patterns.
- **Trade Surveillance**: Tools like NICE Actimize and Smarsh monitor trading activity to detect insider trading, market manipulation, or spoofing. They analyze trading patterns across emails, chats, and voice calls, ensuring compliance with financial conduct regulations.
- **Policy Management**: AI-driven tools generate customized compliance policies based on the latest regulations. They facilitate company-wide policy distribution, employee training, and digital sign-offs to meet audit requirements.

Predictive and Prescriptive Analytics

- **Predictive Compliance Models**: AI algorithms analyze historical compliance issues to predict future violations. They provide early warnings of non-compliance, enabling preemptive measures.
- **Prescriptive Recommendations**: Compliance systems offer prescriptive recommendations on mitigating specific regulatory risks, such as reorganizing business units, modifying accounting practices, or introducing new audit procedures.

Audit Management and Reporting

- **Internal Audit Management**: AI platforms automate internal audits by assessing compliance against pre-set criteria. They identify gaps, suggest corrective actions, and track progress on remediation.
- **External Audit Preparation**: Compliance tools compile necessary documentation and create comprehensive reports for external audits. They reduce audit preparation time by cross-referencing data from financial statements, policy manuals, and transaction records.

Understanding the Financial Legal Landscape

Global Financial Regulations

- **International Financial Reporting Standards (IFRS)**: IFRS sets accounting standards for companies operating globally. These standards cover revenue recognition, leasing, and consolidation, among other areas. AI tools ensure accurate financial statements adhering to IFRS guidelines.
- **Basel Framework**: Basel III outlines global banking regulations concerning capital adequacy, stress testing, and market liquidity. Compliance tools help banks maintain adequate capital and liquidity buffers while managing credit and operational risks.
- **Foreign Account Tax Compliance Act (FATCA)**: FATCA mandates foreign financial institutions to disclose information about U.S. taxpayers holding accounts overseas. Compliance systems streamline client identification, withholding tax processing, and information reporting.

Regional Regulatory Frameworks

- **European Union**: The EU's MiFID II (Markets in Financial Instruments Directive) and GDPR (General Data Protection Regulation) significantly impact financial businesses. MiFID II requires increased transparency in trading, while GDPR imposes stringent data privacy standards. Compliance platforms monitor EU regulatory updates to help companies adapt.

- **United States**: U.S. regulations like the Dodd-Frank Act and Sarbanes-Oxley Act (SOX) govern financial markets and corporate governance, respectively. AI tools ensure compliance by monitoring transactions, executive compensation, and accounting controls.
- **Asia-Pacific**: Regulatory frameworks vary widely across APAC countries, including China's Securities Law, India's SEBI regulations, and Australia's Anti-Money Laundering/Counter-Terrorism Financing (AML/CTF) Act. AI platforms tailor compliance efforts to these specific jurisdictions.

Industry-Specific Regulations

- **Banking**: Banking institutions face regulations covering capital adequacy, AML compliance, and customer privacy. Basel III, the Bank Secrecy Act (BSA), and local banking laws dictate compliance requirements.
- **Investment Management**: Hedge funds, private equity, and mutual funds must adhere to disclosure rules, fiduciary duties, and investor protections. SEC regulations, the Investment Advisers Act, and UCITS guidelines govern this industry.
- **Insurance**: Insurance companies comply with regulations around risk assessment, capital reserves, and policyholder rights. Solvency II, the NAIC Model Laws, and regional frameworks impact operations.

Conclusion

Navigating financial regulations demands constant vigilance and strategic planning. With AI tools for regulatory compliance and predictive analytics, businesses can stay abreast of evolving rules, automate compliance processes, and prepare for audits effectively. Understanding the legal landscape provides clarity on global, regional, and industry-specific frameworks, which are crucial for developing comprehensive compliance strategies. Incorporating these practices into your "Fast Track to Freedom" journey ensures a secure financial future free from regulatory pitfalls.

Part VI: Maintaining and Expanding Financial Freedom

Chapter 27: The Sustainability of Financial Freedom

Achieving financial independence is a remarkable milestone, but sustaining and expanding wealth over time requires deliberate and consistent strategies. This chapter discusses approaches for maintaining financial freedom in the long run, from smart wealth management practices to the importance of continuous learning and adaptability.

Long-term Strategies to Maintain and Expand Wealth

Diversified Investment Portfolios

- **Reassessing Asset Allocation**: As you reach financial goals and life circumstances change, regularly review your portfolio to ensure it reflects your evolving risk tolerance and objectives. Diversification across stocks, bonds, real estate, and alternative investments is crucial.

- **Alternative Investments**: Allocate a portion of your portfolio to alternative investments like private equity, commodities, hedge funds, or infrastructure. These investments often have lower correlations with traditional assets, providing protection during market downturns.

- **Dividends and Passive Income**: Focus on investments that offer stable, passive income streams, such as dividend-paying stocks, real estate, and income-generating digital assets. These can help cover living expenses and ensure your portfolio continues to grow.

Financial Planning and Risk Management

- **Insurance Coverage**: Comprehensive insurance plans (health, life, disability, and property) help protect your wealth in emergencies. Review policies annually to make sure you have adequate coverage.

- **Emergency Funds**: Maintain a cash reserve that covers 6-12 months of living expenses. This buffer protects you from unexpected job loss, market downturns, or medical emergencies.

- **Estate Planning**: Create a detailed estate plan with the help of financial advisors and estate lawyers. Strategies like setting up trusts or gifting assets to heirs can minimize taxes and ensure your wealth is distributed according to your wishes.

Tax Efficiency

- **Tax-Loss Harvesting**: Offset taxable gains by strategically selling underperforming investments. Reinvest proceeds in similar assets to maintain your target asset allocation.

- **Retirement Accounts**: Maximize tax-advantaged retirement accounts, such as 401(k)s and IRAs. Contribute the annual maximum and consider catch-up contributions if you're over 50.

- **Charitable Giving**: Reduce tax liability through charitable giving strategies like donor-advised funds or Qualified Charitable Distributions (QCDs). They help support causes you care about while minimizing estate taxes.

Evolving Wealth-Building Strategies

- **Reinvesting Profits**: As you generate profits from your investments or businesses, reinvest them in new opportunities rather than letting them sit idle. This approach accelerates wealth accumulation.
- **Scaling Businesses**: Identify scalable aspects of your business that can generate exponential growth. Explore expansion into new markets or services and leverage technology for efficient operations.
- **Networking**: Maintain relationships with investors, mentors, and business partners. A strong network provides access to valuable insights and opportunities to expand your wealth.

Continuous Learning and Adaptation Strategies

Financial Education

- **Personal Development**: Stay updated with financial literature, blogs, and courses. Topics like behavioral finance, tax strategies, and macroeconomic trends can reveal new opportunities.
- **Mentorship and Coaching**: Seek mentors who have achieved financial freedom and are willing to share their experiences. Financial coaches offer accountability and fresh perspectives.
- **Workshops and Conferences**: Attend seminars or webinars on wealth-building topics to gain insights into emerging trends, new investment tools, and networking opportunities.

Adaptation to Market Changes

- **Market Research**: Monitor global markets and economic conditions regularly. Stay aware of macroeconomic trends, sector performance, and market sentiment to adjust your portfolio proactively.
- **Tech Disruption**: New technologies can disrupt industries, affecting business strategies and investment landscapes. Stay abreast of tech advancements, particularly in fintech, AI, and blockchain.
- **Agile Pivoting**: When strategies underperform or new opportuni-

ties emerge, pivot quickly. For instance, if a particular gig economy job loses traction, redirect efforts toward a more profitable niche.

Building Resilience

- **Mindset and Emotional Intelligence**: Develop a growth mindset that embraces learning from failures and sees setbacks as opportunities for growth. Emotional intelligence is key in making rational investment decisions.
- **Diversified Skills**: Acquire new skills to adapt to changes in the job market or business landscape. Proficiency in coding, data analysis, or digital marketing can open new income streams.
- **Holistic Wellness**: Prioritize health and well-being through exercise, nutrition, and mental health practices. Financial independence is most meaningful when coupled with physical vitality.

Conclusion

Sustaining financial freedom requires a comprehensive approach that blends strategic financial management with adaptability and continuous learning. By diversifying investments, implementing robust risk management practices, and cultivating the right mindset, you can protect and expand your wealth over time. Embrace lifelong learning, nurture networks, and maintain a proactive, agile approach to navigate future financial challenges and opportunities successfully.

Chapter 28: Philanthropy and Ethical Wealth

Philanthropy and ethical wealth management are crucial components of financial freedom, transforming the pursuit of wealth from a personal goal to a tool for societal good. By intentionally incorporating philanthropy and ethical investing into your financial plan, you can create sustainable value beyond your own life. This chapter explores how to use your wealth to positively impact society and guide your investments according to ethical principles.

Using Wealth for Social Good

Philanthropic Mindset

- **Giving with Purpose**: Effective philanthropy begins with a clear purpose. Determine which causes resonate most with you, whether it's education, healthcare, environmental conservation, or poverty alleviation. Establishing a focused mission can lead to more meaningful contributions.
- **Impactful Giving Strategies**: Strategize your philanthropic efforts

for maximum impact. This could mean donating directly to specific projects, funding research initiatives, or supporting capacity-building for non-profits.

- **Involving the Next Generation**: Engage your family in philanthropic endeavors. By involving children and future heirs, you can instill values of generosity and equip them to continue your legacy of giving.

Philanthropic Vehicles

- **Donor-Advised Funds (DAFs)**: DAFs allow you to donate assets to a fund while receiving immediate tax benefits. The assets grow tax-free and can be distributed to charities over time. They offer flexibility and ease of management.
- **Charitable Trusts**: Charitable remainder trusts provide beneficiaries with income for a specified term before donating the remaining assets to charity. Charitable lead trusts work inversely, supporting a charity first and eventually passing assets to heirs.
- **Direct Giving**: Contributions to nonprofits or individuals in need can have immediate impacts. Consider partnering with local organizations or initiating your own grassroots efforts.

Corporate Social Responsibility (CSR)

- **Aligning Business with Values**: If you own a business, consider integrating CSR into its mission. Implement ethical labor practices, reduce the environmental footprint, and support community projects to enhance the company's positive influence.
- **Employee Engagement**: Foster a culture of giving by involving employees in CSR initiatives. Match their donations, provide paid volunteer opportunities, and encourage innovative projects.
- **Public-Private Partnerships**: Collaborate with governments or other businesses to tackle complex social challenges. Pooling resources can amplify the effectiveness of your philanthropy.

Ethical Investing and Its Impacts

Principles of Ethical Investing

- **ESG Factors**: Ethical investing often revolves around ESG (Environmental, Social, and Governance) principles. This means evaluating companies based on their sustainability practices, social responsibility, and corporate governance.
- **Socially Responsible Investing (SRI)**: SRI focuses on avoiding investments that harm society, like tobacco, gambling, or weapons manufacturing. Instead, it emphasizes funding companies that promote positive social values.
- **Impact Investing**: Impact investing seeks investments that deliver measurable social or environmental benefits alongside financial returns. Examples include affordable housing, renewable energy, and financial inclusion.

Impact on Portfolio Management

- **Risk and Return**: Ethical investing can lower exposure to companies facing significant ESG risks. Businesses with strong ESG practices tend to have better long-term risk management, reducing the likelihood of fines, lawsuits, or reputational damage.
- **Active Management**: Portfolio managers focusing on ethical investments engage directly with companies to advocate for improved ESG practices. This activism can help drive corporate change from within.
- **Long-term Trends**: Ethical investments are often aligned with emerging economic trends. Investments in renewable energy or green technologies may benefit from increasing global climate action and regulatory support.

Building an Ethical Portfolio

- **ESG Ratings and Screeners**: ESG rating agencies like MSCI and Sustainalytics provide comprehensive assessments of companies' ESG practices. Use these ratings to screen investments that align with your ethical priorities.

- **Thematic Funds**: Many mutual funds and exchange-traded funds (ETFs) now focus specifically on ESG, impact investing, or SRI themes. Choose funds that align with your values while meeting financial goals.
- **Community Investments**: Support community development initiatives through investments in affordable housing projects, microfinance institutions, or local cooperative ventures.

Challenges and Criticisms

- **Greenwashing**: Be wary of companies that exaggerate or falsely claim to be environmentally friendly. Scrutinize their ESG practices and rely on credible third-party assessments.
- **Performance Myths**: Ethical investments have sometimes been criticized for underperforming compared to traditional investments. However, research shows that ESG-focused companies often deliver competitive, long-term returns.

Conclusion

Incorporating philanthropy and ethical wealth management into your financial plan transforms wealth-building into a force for good. Philanthropic strategies allow you to share your success with those in need, while ethical investing promotes sustainable business practices that benefit society and the environment. As you pursue financial independence, remember that true freedom is the ability to leave a legacy of positive change and use your resources to build a better world.

Chapter 29: Mentoring and Community Building

Financial freedom is not an end but a journey that becomes richer when shared with others. Mentoring and community building provide opportunities to give back, shape the next generation of entrepreneurs, and create support networks that uplift everyone involved. This chapter focuses on the importance of giving back through knowledge sharing and fostering communities that empower individuals toward mutual growth and success.

Giving Back Through Knowledge Sharing

Becoming a Mentor

- **Assess Your Strengths**: Identify the areas where your skills and experiences are most valuable. Your unique path to financial independence offers insights into challenges faced by those starting their journey.

- **Understanding Mentee Needs**: Recognize that each mentee has distinct goals and challenges. Build a relationship based on listening and understanding their specific needs before providing guidance.

- **Customized Mentorship**: Craft mentorship sessions tailored to each individual's learning style and pace. Some may benefit from structured lessons, while others thrive in informal, conversational settings.

Structuring Effective Mentorship Programs

- **Mentorship Frameworks**: A structured framework ensures consistency in mentoring sessions. Develop goals, milestones, and timelines that mentees can use to track their progress.

- **Cross-Disciplinary Learning**: Encourage mentees to explore a broad range of subjects. Financial independence often requires multidisciplinary skills, including marketing, negotiation, and personal development.

- **Feedback and Improvement**: Regularly gather feedback from mentees to refine the mentorship process. Use this input to adjust your approach, keeping it relevant and effective.

Knowledge Sharing Platforms

- **Workshops and Webinars**: Host workshops or webinars covering topics like financial literacy, business development, or investment strategies. Record and share these sessions online to reach a broader audience.
- **Online Courses**: Create digital courses that provide step-by-step guidance in specific fields. Course platforms can help you reach learners globally and monetize your content.
- **Written Resources**: Write blogs, eBooks, or guides that reflect your expertise and experience. These resources are invaluable for individuals who prefer self-paced learning.

Building Networks and Communities for Support and Growth

The Value of Networks

- **Collaborative Opportunities**: Networks introduce you to individuals with complementary skills, enabling business collaborations, partnerships, or joint investments.
- **Market Insights**: Accessing diverse perspectives helps you identify market trends and investment opportunities that may otherwise go unnoticed.
- **Peer Accountability**: Supportive networks hold you accountable to your financial and professional goals. Regular check-ins with trusted peers keep you motivated and focused.

Building a Supportive Community

- **Shared Purpose**: Foster communities around shared values and goals. A common purpose ensures that members are aligned, leading to authentic and supportive interactions.
- **Leadership and Structure**: Strong community leadership provides

structure while ensuring that every member has a voice. Designate clear roles and responsibilities for smooth operations.

- **Inclusive Culture**: Encourage diversity in membership, bringing together people from various backgrounds and industries. Emphasize empathy, respect, and collaboration to build a safe environment.

Community Platforms

- **Social Media Groups**: Create and manage groups on social media platforms like Facebook or LinkedIn to facilitate online conversations. Engage members through polls, Q&A sessions, and interactive discussions.

- **Meetups and Conferences**: Host virtual or in-person meetups to bring community members together. Annual conferences or summits are ideal for sharing in-depth insights, celebrating achievements, and building deeper connections.

- **Membership Sites**: Build membership sites where community members can access exclusive resources, events, and coaching services. Encourage content contributions from experienced members.

The Ripple Effect of Community Impact

- **Amplifying Reach**: An active, vibrant community can amplify your reach and influence, helping spread financial literacy, business insights, and investment strategies beyond individual mentorships.

- **Paying It Forward**: Encourage mentees and community members to mentor others in their networks, creating a positive cycle of giving back and personal growth.

- **Legacy Building**: Through mentoring and community building, you help shape the financial future of many others. This legacy can impact future generations and contribute to broader societal improvement.

Conclusion

Mentoring and community building are powerful methods to give back while creating a robust network that enriches everyone involved. By sharing knowledge and fostering collaboration, you can unlock doors to success for others while reinforcing your values and personal growth. Ultimately, these practices help build a legacy of empowerment, ensuring that financial freedom leads to widespread opportunities for support and advancement.

Influencers to follow:

Grant Cardone

Alex Hormozi

Napolean Hill

Dan Pena

Chapter 30: Health and Wellness in Wealth Building

In the quest for financial freedom, it's crucial to recognize the symbiotic relationship between wealth and well-being. Prioritizing personal health and wellness creates a strong foundation that enables you to enjoy financial success while minimizing burnout and stress. This chapter explores the significance of balancing financial pursuits with personal well-being and provides practical tools and practices for maintaining physical and mental health.

Balancing Financial Pursuits with Personal Well-being

Defining Balance

- **Work-Life Integration:** Strive for a harmonious integration of professional and personal responsibilities. Recognize that wealth-building activities should coexist with family time, hobbies, and relaxation.

- **Sustainable Productivity**: Replace the 'hustle and grind' mentality with a sustainable approach to productivity. Work efficiently, avoiding the burnout that often accompanies overworking.
- **Mindful Financial Goals**: Set financial goals aligned with your values and aspirations. Pursue goals that enhance your life quality, rather than sacrificing well-being for purely financial milestones.

Identifying Stressors

- **Self-Awareness**: Regularly check in with yourself to identify stressors affecting your productivity or health. These could be unrealistic deadlines, difficult clients, or unnecessary financial pressures.
- **Boundary Setting**: Establish boundaries to protect your time and energy. For instance, schedule 'off' hours where you disconnect from work-related emails or client requests.
- **Delegating Tasks**: Recognize tasks that can be delegated to free up your time and energy for essential activities. Delegation can also enhance business efficiency by allowing others to contribute their strengths.

Financial Wellness Practices

- **Emergency Funds**: Establish an emergency fund to cover three to six months of living expenses. This financial cushion reduces anxiety during unexpected situations like job loss or medical emergencies.
- **Debt Management**: Create a debt reduction plan that prioritizes high-interest debts first. Managing debt responsibly alleviates financial strain and improves credit health.
- **Income Diversification**: Build multiple streams of income to mitigate risks associated with market volatility or business downturns. Diversified income streams also offer a more stable financial base.

Tools and Practices for Mental and Physical Health

Mental Health Practices

- **Meditation and Mindfulness**: Practice meditation or mindfulness daily to cultivate focus, reduce anxiety, and improve clarity. Guided meditation apps or simple breathing exercises are effective tools.

- **Journaling**: Journaling is a therapeutic way to process thoughts, feelings, and stressors. Regularly writing about your goals, challenges, and gratitude helps promote mental clarity.

- **Support Systems**: Lean on trusted friends, mentors, or therapists who can provide emotional support. Building meaningful connections helps create a sense of belonging and validation.

Physical Health Practices

- **Exercise and Movement**: Engage in physical activities that you enjoy, whether it's running, yoga, swimming, or dancing. Regular exercise boosts mood, improves sleep, and enhances energy levels.

- **Nutrition and Hydration**: Prioritize balanced meals rich in fruits, vegetables, lean proteins, and healthy fats. Staying hydrated is equally crucial for optimal cognitive and physical functioning.

- **Sleep Hygiene**: Establish a consistent sleep schedule and minimize screen usage before bed. Quality sleep strengthens the immune system, improves concentration, and helps the body recover.

Tech Tools for Wellness

- **Wearable Devices**: Fitness trackers and smartwatches monitor daily activity levels, heart rate, and sleep quality. These metrics offer insights to adjust exercise and sleeping patterns.

- **Mental Health Apps**: Numerous apps provide guided meditations, cognitive behavioral therapy techniques, and stress-relief exercises. These tools can complement your mental health care routine.

- **Nutritional Tracking**: Nutrition apps track caloric intake and identify nutritional deficiencies, helping users plan balanced diets and reach fitness goals.

Conclusion

Health and wellness are essential pillars for long-term wealth building. By prioritizing mental and physical well-being, you create a sustainable lifestyle that enables you to fully enjoy your financial achievements. Maintaining a healthy balance allows you to pursue financial goals with intention while living a life that is physically energized, mentally focused, and emotionally fulfilling. Incorporate these tools and practices into your daily routine to build an abundant future without compromising your most valuable asset—your well-being.

Top Health book recommended "The Kidney Friendly Diet"

Health plan:

-drink Ginger Tea

-Cut all sugar out

-cut all preservative foods out

-eat 90%- 96% ground beef

-drink Alkaline 9.5 PH water or osmosis water

-Meat is the best option

-Onions

Chapter 31: The Future of Financial Freedom

The rapidly evolving financial landscape, powered by technological advancements and shifting global trends, will significantly impact the path to financial freedom in the coming years. Understanding these emerging trends and preparing for future challenges can position individuals to seize unprecedented opportunities in wealth-building. This final chapter explores emerging trends in finance and technology, as well as strategies to future-proof your financial journey.

Emerging Trends in Finance and Technology

The Rise of Decentralized Finance (DeFi)

- **Blockchain and Smart Contracts**: Blockchain technology and smart contracts enable transparent, peer-to-peer transactions without traditional intermediaries. DeFi platforms use these technologies to provide decentralized lending, borrowing, and trading services.

- **Decentralized Exchanges**: Decentralized exchanges (DEXs) are platforms that enable users to trade cryptocurrencies directly, giving them control over their assets without custodial risks.

- **Tokenized Assets**: Tokenization allows traditional assets like real estate and commodities to be traded as blockchain-based tokens. This unlocks liquidity and fractional ownership, making high-value assets more accessible.

AI-Driven Financial Insights

- **Predictive Analytics**: Artificial Intelligence (AI) models are increasingly able to analyze vast datasets for market trends and investment opportunities, allowing for more accurate predictions of stock or cryptocurrency prices.
- **Robo-Advisors**: Robo-advisors leverage AI algorithms to provide personalized financial advice at a lower cost. They help optimize portfolios, adjust risk levels, and rebalance investments automatically.
- **AI for Risk Management**: AI tools identify potential risks by analyzing historical data, financial documents, and market indicators. This is particularly valuable in insurance, compliance, and credit risk assessment.

Expanding Gig Economy

- **Flexible Work Platforms**: The gig economy provides digital platforms where individuals can find freelancing and contract work that offers higher flexibility than traditional employment.
- **Skill-Based Opportunities**: As demand for specialized skills increases, freelancers can earn premium rates by offering their expertise in areas like graphic design, programming, digital marketing, or AI development.
- **Remote Collaboration**: Enhanced remote collaboration tools enable seamless team management, increasing productivity for gig workers and businesses alike.

Digital Currencies and Central Bank Digital Currencies (CBDCs)

- **Cryptocurrency Adoption**: Growing acceptance of cryptocurrencies and stablecoins for everyday transactions opens new possibilities for decentralized finance, cross-border payments, and financial inclusion.
- **Central Bank Digital Currencies**: Governments and central banks worldwide are exploring digital versions of their national

currencies to complement traditional fiat money. CBDCs aim to streamline monetary policy, payments, and regulatory oversight.

Financial Inclusivity and Accessibility

- **Mobile Banking**: Mobile banking is growing rapidly, providing financial services to millions globally who lack access to traditional banks. It facilitates savings, remittances, and microloans.
- **Financial Literacy Tools**: Innovative apps and online courses empower individuals to learn about budgeting, saving, investing, and financial planning.
- **Micro-Investment Platforms**: Micro-investment platforms allow users to invest in fractional shares, lowering the entry barriers for investing and wealth-building.

Preparing for Future Challenges and Opportunities in Wealth Building

Continuous Learning and Skill Development

- **Staying Current**: Continuously update your knowledge on emerging trends like blockchain, AI, and digital currencies. Follow thought leaders, attend webinars, and read industry reports.
- **Learning New Skills**: Diversify your skill set by learning skills like coding, data analysis, or content creation. Such skills open doors to emerging digital opportunities.

Diversification and Adaptability

- **Portfolio Diversification**: Diversify your investment portfolio across various asset classes and regions. Consider a mix of traditional and alternative assets, including cryptocurrencies and real estate.
- **Agility and Flexibility**: Remain agile in your financial strategies by regularly reviewing goals and adjusting plans based on market conditions or technological changes.

Cybersecurity and Data Privacy

- **Data Protection**: Use secure passwords, two-factor authentication, and encryption to protect sensitive financial data.
- **Fraud Prevention**: Stay vigilant against phishing, fraud, and scams. Monitor your credit report and financial transactions regularly.

Ethical and Sustainable Investing

- **ESG Investing**: Environmental, Social, and Governance (ESG) investing aligns financial goals with values by prioritizing companies that demonstrate ethical and sustainable practices.
- **Social Impact Investments**: Invest in businesses or projects that aim to address global challenges like climate change, healthcare, or poverty alleviation.

Conclusion

The future of financial freedom will be shaped by dynamic technological advancements and changing global trends. By understanding emerging trends and proactively developing new skills, individuals can prepare for the challenges and opportunities that lie ahead. Staying informed and adaptable will help you navigate this new financial era, empowering you to build a resilient, forward-thinking path to lasting wealth.

Future Financial plan and how to continue to grow it:

Message from the Author:

I hope you enjoyed this book, I love astrology and knew there was not a book such as this out on the shelf. I love metaphysical items as well. Please check out my other books:

-Life of Government Benefits

-My life of Hell

-My life with Hydrocephalus

-Red Sky

-World Domination:Woman's rule

-World Domination:Woman's Rule 2: The War

-Life and Banishment of Apophis: book 1

-The Kidney Friendly Diet

-The Ultimate Hemp Cookbook

-Creating a Dispensary(legally)

-Cleanliness throughout life: the importance of showering from childhood to adulthood.

-Strong Roots: The Risks of Overcoddling children

-Hemp Horoscopes: Cosmic Insights and Earthly Healing

- Celestial Hemp Navigating the Zodiac: Through the Green Cosmos

-Astrological Hemp: Aligning The Stars with Earth's Ancient Herb

-The Astrological Guide to Hemp: Stars, Signs, and Sacred Leaves

-Green Growth: Innovative Marketing Strategies for your Hemp Products and Dispensary

-Cosmic Cannabis

-Astrological Munchies

-Henry The Hemp

-Zodiacal Roots: The Astrological Soul Of Hemp

- **Green Constellations: Intersection of Hemp and Zodiac**

-Hemp in The Houses: An astrological Adventure Through The Cannabis Galaxy

-Galactic Ganja Guide

Heavenly Hemp

Zodiac Leaves
Doctor Who Astrology
Cannastrology
Stellar Satvias and Cosmic Indicas
Celestial Cannabis: A Zodiac Journey
AstroHerbology: The Sky and The Soil: Volume 1
AstroHerbology:Celestial Cannabis:Volume 2
Cosmic Cannabis Cultivation
The Starry Guide to Herbal Harmony: Volume 1
The Starry Guide to Herbal Harmony: Cannabis Universe: Volume 2
Yugioh Astrology: Astrological Guide to Deck, Duels and more
Nightmare Mansion: Echoes of The Abyss
Nightmare Mansion 2: Legacy of Shadows
Nightmare Mansion 3: Shadows of the Forgotten
Nightmare Mansion 4: Echoes of the Damned
The Life and Banishment of Apophis: Book 2
Nightmare Mansion: Halls of Despair
Healing with Herb: Cannabis and Hydrocephalus
Planetary Pot: Aligning with Astrological Herbs: Volume 1

Check out my Virtual dispensary for all your hemp needs: https://shift.store/sg1fan23477/retail

If you want solar for your home go here: https://www.harborsolar.live/apophisenterprises/

Instagrams:
@apophis_enterprises,
@hempkingdom2024,
 @apophisbookemporium,
@apophisfashion,
@apophisscardshop
Twitter: @apophisenterpr1, Tiktok:@apophisenterprise
Youtube: @sg1fan23477 Top of Form
Podcast: Apophis Chat Zone: https://open.spotify.com/show/5zXbrCLEV2xzCp8ybrfHsk?si=fb4d4fdbdce44dec
Newsletter: https://apophiss-newsletter-27c897.beehiiv.com/

9 798869 364869